Pain, Death, and the Law

Law, Meaning, and Violence

The scope of Law, Meaning, and Violence is defined by the wide-ranging scholarly debates signaled by each of the words in the title. Those debates have taken place among and between lawyers, anthropologists, political theorists, sociologists, and historians, as well as literary and cultural critics. This series is intended to recognize the importance of such ongoing conversations about law, meaning, and violence as well as to encourage and further them.

Series Editors:

Martha Minow, Harvard Law School
Elaine Scarry, Harvard University
Austin Sarat, Amherst College

Pain, Death, and the Law

Edited by
Austin Sarat

Ann Arbor
THE UNIVERSITY OF MICHIGAN PRESS

Copyright © by the University of Michigan 2001
All rights reserved
Published in the United States of America by
The University of Michigan Press
Manufactured in the United States of America
⊗ Printed on acid-free paper

2004   2003   2002   2001   4   3   2   1

A CIP catalog record for this book is available from the British Library.

Library of Congress Cataloging-in-Publication Data

Pain, death, and the law / edited by Austin Sarat.
       p.   cm. — (Law, meaning, and violence)
    ISBN 0-472-09767-9 (cloth : acid-free paper) — ISBN 0-472-06767-2
(paper : acid-free paper)
       1. Capital punishment—United States.   2. Body, Human—Law and
legislation—United States.   3. Pain—Social aspects.   I. Sarat,
Austin.   II. Series.
    KF9227.C2 P35   2001
    345.73'0773—dc21   00-012320

Contents

Introduction: On Pain and Death as Facts of Legal Life

Austin Sarat

[T]he law reveals itself for what it is: less the command that has
death as its sanction, than death itself wearing the face of law. . . .
The law kills. Death is always the horizon of the law: if you do this,
you will die.

—Maurice Blanchot (*The Step Not Beyond,* 24–25)

"Legal interpretation plays on a field of pain and death." These are the
words with which Robert Cover began "Violence and the Word."[1] That
essay was designed to reorient legal theory, or at least to remind legal
scholars eagerly pursuing the interpretive turn or the parallels between
law and literature of the base materiality of the legal enterprise. While
Cover's work is now regarded as something of a classic in contemporary legal thought,[2] surprisingly few scholars have taken up his invita-
tion to explore the intimate connections among pain, death, and the
law.[3] The scholarship collected here is intended to serve as something
of a corrective to that fact. It puts pain and death at the center of think-

---

1. Robert Cover, "Violence and the Word," *Yale Law Journal* 95 (1986): 1601.

2. As Jonathan Simon puts it, "Cover's 'Violence and the Word' still haunts us a
decade later in part because it sounded such a dissonant note in the intellectual trends of
its time. . . . The great value of 'Violence and the Word' is precisely in its alarming insistence that law's violence be acknowledged, not just at the extremities of the legal order,
but at the center of the process in judicial interpretation." See "The Vicissitudes of Law's
Violence," typescript, 1998, 10.

3. For exceptions see Austin Sarat and Thomas R. Kearns, "A Journey through Forgetting: Toward a Jurisprudence of Violence," in *The Fate of Law,* ed. Austin Sarat and
Thomas R. Kearns (Ann Arbor: University of Michigan Press, 1991); and Desmond Manderson, ed. *Courting Death: The Law of Mortality* (London: Pluto Press, 1999).

ing about law, highlighting the way law imagines the body in pain as well as the way pain and death become jurisprudential facts.

As Cover correctly observed, despite their undeniable significance, pain and death have played little role, and occupied little space, in legal theory and jurisprudence.[4] Or, when they are present, awareness of the pain or death done, or authorized, by officials are divorced from acts of interpretation, as if the act of speaking or writing the words of law could be separated from the inscription of those words on the bodies of citizens.[5] By failing to confront law's lethal character and the masking of its interpretive violence, legal theory tacitly encourages officials to ignore the bloody consequences of their authoritative acts and the pain those acts produce. Moreover, by equating the conditions of legal legitimacy with that masking, much of legal theory promotes righteous indifference and allows pain and death to proceed unabated. Law, surrounded by so much pain and death, is, nonetheless, able to maintain its calm, bureaucratic facade.

Neither traditional nor critical jurisprudence have truly come to terms with the fact that the business of law, when everything else is said and done, is a painful, often deadly one, that legal interpretation is frequently a preface to the use of physical force, and that law traffics in pain and death with such cool efficiency. The pain and death that law dispenses are generally invisible in both what might be called law's "official story," and many of its critical counternarratives.[6]

In law's official story judges are bound, more or less tightly, compelled, more or less directly, by its rules and the only accountability that is demanded is accountability within the terms of those rules.[7] That story quiets the pain and death in which law deals through its self-proclaimed, neutral concern with rules and rule following. As Olivecrona puts it,

---

4. Cover, "Violence and the Word." See also Tom Dumm, "The Fear of Law," *Studies in Law, Politics, and Society* 10 (1990): 29.

5. Cover himself divorces interpretation from violence as if the latter were merely a matter of implementation or a defect of administration. See "Violence and the Word."

6. It is true, of course, that violence and law have sometimes been tied together in a definitional sense. See Alf Ross, *On Law and Justice* (Berkeley and Los Angeles: University of California Press, 1959), 34; Hans Kelsen, *General Theory of Law and State*, trans. Anders Wedberg (New York: Russell and Russell, 1945); Noberto Bobbio, "Law & Force," *Monist* 48 (1965): 321.

7. For a discussion of this view see Robert Ferguson, "The Judicial Opinion as a Literary Genre," *Yale Journal of Law and the Humanities* 2 (1990): 201.

Actual violence is . . . kept very much in the background. . . . Such
a state of things is apt to create the belief that violence is alien to the
law, or of secondary importance. This is, however, a fatal illusion.
. . . [Law's] real character is largely obscured and this is done by
means of metaphysical ideas and expressions. It is not bluntly said,
e.g. that the function of the courts is to determine the use of force.
Instead their function is said to be the "administration of justice"
or the ascertaining of "rights" and "duties."[8]

Law's official story traditionally has been preoccupied with law's
majesty rather than its monstrousness,[9] with its value-declaring, rights-
enhancing, community-building aspects[10] rather than its "monopoly of
legitimate violence."[11] It has failed to take seriously the fact that those
who control and dispense pain and death and those against whom they
dispense it

undergo achingly disparate . . . experiences. For the . . . [former],
. . . pain and fear are remote, unreal and largely unshared. They
are, therefore, almost never made part of the interpretive artifact,
such as the judicial opinion. On the other hand, for those who
impose the violence, the justification is important, real and carefully cultivated. Conversely, for the victim, the justification for the

---

8. See Karl Olivecrona, *Law as Fact* (Copenhagen: Einer Munksgaard, 1939), 125
and 127. For an exception see Justice Holmes's opinion in *American Banana Co. v. United
Fruit Co.*, 213 U.S. 347, 356 (1908). Holmes said, "Law is a statement of circumstances in
which the public force will be brought to bear upon man through the courts." However,
as Minow, argues, "[J]udges and top level bureaucrats do not have to see violence. Their
jobs are structured so violence happens well down the chain of command, and they often
have no point of reference for acknowledging the violence they hear others describe." See
Martha Minow, "Words and the Door to the Land of Change: Law, Language, and Family Violence," typescript, 1990, 14.

9. Michel Foucault argues that in political and legal theory "the King remains the
central personage in the whole legal edifice of the West." See *Power/Knowledge*, trans.
Colin Gordon, Leo Marshall, John Mepham, and Kate Soper (New York: Pantheon, 1980),
94.

10. See Robert Cover, "Nomos and Narrative," *Harvard Law Review* 97 (1983): 4.

11. The phrase "the monopoly of legitimate violence" is used by Max Weber. See
From Max Weber: Essays in Sociology, ed. and trans. H. H. Gerth and C. Wright Mills (New
York: Oxford University Press, 1946), 78. See also Rudolph von Ihering, *Law as a Means to
an End* (Boston: Boston Books, 1913), 230–46.

violence recedes in reality and significance in proportion to the overwhelming reality of the pain and fear that is suffered.[12]

The critical tradition in contemporary jurisprudence challenges the distinction between law and politics, questions the ability of language to govern human will, and acknowledges the symbolic violence of legal interpretation, but it hardly does much better in acknowledging and taking seriously pain and death as facts of legal life. Critics, like their mainstream counterparts, privilege adjudication.[13] However, instead of celebrating law's majesty, critics focus on its complicity in legitimating structures of hierarchy, inequality, and oppression.[14] Critics privilege adjudication as the site of law because they see law as a form of consciousness[15] and doctrine as a useful vehicle for understanding the consciousness they wish to change. In this work law loses its claims to distinctiveness and is exposed as a system of power and power relations not unlike many others in society.

For many critics the real violence of law is found in its reification and mystification of social relations.[16] Law is alienating; its violence is cultural and symbolic. Both physical pain and death, and the discursive construction of both as facts of legal life, are quite consciously put aside. Critics leave the full demonstration of law's dealing in pain and death to others. Thus the critical story does little better than law's official story in exploring pain and death as legal phenomena or in explaining the connection between interpretive violence and the violence done to bodies.

Scholars recently have begun to fill this gap. Some have come to

---

12. Cover, "Violence and the Word," 1629 n. 7.

13. This argument is developed by Frank Munger and Carroll Seron, "Critical Legal Studies versus Critical Legal Theory," *Law and Policy* 6 (1984): 257. See also Ed Sparer, "Fundamental Human Rights, Legal Entitlements, and Social Struggles: A Friendly Critique of the Critical Legal Studies Movement," *Stanford Law Review* 36 (1984): 509.

14. See, for example, Duncan Kennedy, "Legal Education as Training for Hierarchy," in *The Politics of Law*, ed. David Kairys (New York: Pantheon, 1982).

15. Robert Gordon, "New Developments in Legal Theory," in *The Politics of Law*, ed. David Kairys (New York: Pantheon, 1982). See also Karl Klare, "Labor Law as Ideology: Toward a New Historiography of Collective Bargaining Law," *Industrial Relations Law Journal* 4 (1981): 450.

16. See Peter Gabel, "Reification in Legal Reasoning," *Research in Law and Sociology* 3 (1980): 25. See also Peter Gabel and Duncan Kennedy, "Roll Over Beethoven," *Stanford Law Review* 36 (1984): 1.

pain and death as part of an interest in the legal construction of bodies.[17] Bodies are everywhere in law. From wrongful death suits to police brutality, from abortion to euthanasia. Surveying this landscape, Hyde claims that "the multiple, competing constructions of the body in American law show the impossibility of knowledge of the body unmediated by discourse. And those constructions . . . are never innocent."[18] Yet not every construction of the body in law requires or involves an acknowledgment of pain and death as facts of legal life. Recognizing the ubiquity of the body in legal discourse, in itself, tells us nothing about when, where, and how law "plays on a field of pain and death."

Hyde surely recognizes this. For him the appearance of pain in legal discourse marks the development of a particular way of understanding the body, what Hyde calls the "sentimentalized body."[19] In his account the sentimentalized body is a site both of differentiation and of empathy. As Hyde puts it, "However sentimental bodies construct difference, the limits of such differentiation—the very essence of constructing a sentimental body—is always that such a body *feels* pain and to that extent may excite what we call *empathy* . . . , for which the contemporary idiom is often precisely 'I feel your pain.'"[20] Recognizing pain as a fact of legal life may be necessary to establish the measure of damages in a tort suit or to impose limits on the kinds of physical punishment that are constitutionally tolerable, but Hyde contends, contra Cover, that the construction of pain provides a bridge between the body constructed in legal discourse and others standing, at least for a moment, beyond the reach of law. Pain figures prominently as a device through which law builds solidarity. Attending to pain, in his view, poses no special challenge for law.

If, according to Hyde, the acknowledgment of pain poses no special challenge to law,[21] the same cannot so easily be claimed when the subject turns to death. Here work by Peter Fitzpatrick is particularly

17. See, for example, Kristin Bumiller, "Real Violence/Body Fictions," typescript, 1992; and Drucilla Cornell, *The Imaginary Domain: Abortion, Pornography, and Sexual Harassment* (New York: Routledge, 1995).

18. Alan Hyde, *Bodies of Law* (Princeton, N.J.: Princeton University Press, 1997), 6.

19. Ibid., 192.

20. Ibid., 193.

21. For a different view see Austin Sarat, "Speaking of Death: Narratives of Violence in Capital Trials," *Law and Society Review* 27 (1993): 19.

instructive.[22] Fitzpatrick argues that death marks the limit of law, being neither containable in, nor contained by, law. Yet this limit is, on his account,

> productively ambivalent. As marking our limit, it is ours. It is of us . . . yet we cannot know or experience the horizon fully because it does mark our limit. It borders and connects us with what is beyond us. But not utterly beyond . . . So we are "bound" to a seeming irresolution of the horizon as a condition and quality of our contained identity and the horizon as opening onto all that lies beyond an identity.[23]

Death is neither external to law, something with which law may of its own accord engage or avoid—as one might think on reading Cover—nor an overdetermining presence inside law. Instead, in Fitz-patrick's view there is a homology between law and death. "Death," he says, "accommodates law's intrinsic claim to fix, determine, and hold life, to deny its circumstance and possibility. . . . Law has an affinity with death or some similarity to it."[24] Moreover, law, like death, brings together "certainty and uncertainty, the determinate and what is beyond determination."[25]

If we are adequately to theorize law, we must think about law in relation to death. "[D]eath is the horizon of law in that death is an hori-zon belonging to law. . . . But the horizon is also a relation between law and death as different and separate."[26] Death marks the limits of law by denying that law can be more than its present facticity. "Death," Fitz-patrick notes, "denies that promise. It effects a closure around the already determined and denies it the ability to be otherwise."[27]

---

22. See Peter Fitzpatrick, "Death as the Horizon of Law," in *Courting Death: The Law of Mortality,* ed. Desmond Manderson (London: Pluto Press, 1999), 19. See also Peter Fitz-patrick, "'Always More to Do': Capital Punishment and the (De)Composition of Law," in *The Killing State: Capital Punishment in Law, Politics, and Culture* (New York: Oxford University Press, 1999).

23. Fitzpatrick, "Always More to Do," 119.

24. Ibid., 120.

25. Ibid. As Manderson puts it, "[L]aw seeks to control every aspect of our lives, including the manner of our passing; while death is precisely that element which lies out-side our control." See Desmond Manderson, "Introduction: Tales from the Crypt—a Metaphor, an Image, a Story," in *Courting Death,* 2.

26. Fitzpatrick, "Death as Horizon," 20.

27. Ibid., 26.

In this effort to bring pain and death to the fore in thinking about law, great importance, and great controversy, attaches to the work of Elaine Scarry.[28] Cover's effort to cultivate a jurisprudence that makes pain and death central to its subject draws heavily on Scarry, as do some of those who have tried to take up his call.[29] Cover, following Scarry, separates pain and language; pain exists outside of language, it has a materiality that language lacks. It is destructive of language itself. As Scarry puts it, pain "actively destroys language . . . bringing about an immediate reversion to a state anterior to language, to the sounds and cries a human being makes before language is learned."[30] Pain for her is a "primary physical act . . . a pure physical experience of negation, an immediate sensory rendering of 'against.'"[31] So great is the priority and power of pain as a fact in the world that Scarry contends there is a "simple and absolute incompatibility of pain and the world."[32]

Scholars have taken Scarry to task for her "naturalistic notion of pain"[33] and for the related failure to historicize its construction.[34] Pain for Scarry is, to use Cover's words, "utterly real," existing outside language, in need of, and indeed resistant to, any linguistic construction.[35] For her critics, in contrast, "the pain that we can know as between ourselves is *in* language. . . . Language is how we live 'in' pain, not in some fantasy of community divorced from it."[36] However, to recognize the linguistic life of pain and of death, one need not say or believe that there is nothing physical, material about these phenomena.

This recognition suggests that pain and death live in and through various institutions and their linguistic practices, institutions and practices that are historically and culturally situated.[37] As Kleinman and Kleinman contend,

---

28. Elaine Scarry, *The Body in Pain: The Making and Unmaking of the World* (New York: Oxford University Press, 1985).

29. See, e.g., Sarat and Kearns, "A Journey through Forgetting."

30. Scarry, *The Body in Pain*, 4.

31. Ibid., 28, 52.

32. Ibid., 50.

33. See Peter Fitzpatrick, "Why the Law is Also Non-Violent," typescript, 1999, 8.

34. Roselyne Rey, *The History of Pain*, trans. Louise Elliott Wallace, J. A. Cadden, and S. W. Cadden (Cambridge: Harvard University Press, 1995). Also see Mary Jo DelVecchio Good et al., eds., *Pain as Human Experience: Anthropological Perspectives* (Berkeley and Los Angeles: University of California Press, 1992).

35. Cover, "Violence and the Word," 1609 n. 20.

36. Fitzpatrick, "Why Law Is Non-Violent," 32, 33.

37. "Only an excessive allegiance to a referential theory of language would lead us to privilege its pointing function in relation to experiences like pain. . . . [S]uch a theory

It is important to avoid essentializing, naturalizing, or sentimentalizing suffering. There is no single way to suffer; there is no timeless or spaceless universal shape to suffering. There are communi-
ties in which suffering is devalued and others in which it is
endowed with utmost significance. The meanings and modes of
suffering have been shown by historians and anthropologists alike
to be greatly diverse.[38]

Pain and death make sense to us in different ways in different historical periods and in different cultures.

Taken together the essays collected in this book indicate that, in contemporary America, law provides one of the key sites to examine the
situation of pain and death, just as taking pain and death seriously
helps us understand the situation of law. *Pain, Death, and the Law* is
premised on the belief that if we are to make progress in grasping the
intimate connections of these three terms of our social existence we
need grounded studies, research that proceeds at a somewhat lower
level of abstraction than the invaluable work already done by scholars
like Hyde and Fitzpatrick. Thus the essays collected in this volume con-
centrate on cases in which pain and death are, at least in one sense,
close at hand, cases in which the law traffics in punishment, sometimes
deadly punishment, or in which the law is asked to sanction a right to
die. There are, of course, other legal arenas to which one might turn to
explore law's relation to pain and death, for example, wrongful death
litigation, legal responses to domestic violence and the use of lethal
force by the police, each of which would provide a valuable and illuminating perspective of that relation. This book is thus less of a survey
or comprehensive treatment than an effort to move legal scholarship by
focusing on a couple of areas in which law, pain, and death seem particularly intimately connected, to mark a path for inquiry that might, in
the future, be extended.

---

would have no place for the performative aspects of language, or for the role of the
speech genre of a society to mold the experience of suffering so that certain experiences
of pain and grieving become expressible while others are shrouded in silence." See
Arthur Kleinman, Veena Das, and Margaret Locke, "Introduction: Social Suffering,"
Daedalus 125 (1996): xiv.

    38. Arthur Kleinman and Joan Kleinman, "The Appeal of Experience; the Dismay of
Images: Cultural Appropriations of Suffering in Our Times," *Daedalus* 125 (1996): 2.

Like both the official and critical accounts of law discussed above, *Pain, Death, and the Law* takes as its object of study judicial opinions. But in the analysis of those opinions the contributors are particularly concerned to explore the pain and death that sit on, as well as below, the surface of law.[39] They recognize that pain "is not that inexpressible something that destroys communication or marks an exit from one's existence in language. Instead it makes a claim asking for acknowledgment, which may be given or denied."[40] They treat law as one domain to which such claims are addressed.

Moreover, they do not regard pain and death as objective facts of a universe remote from law; rather they examine how both are discursively constructed in and by law and how both help to construct and give meaning to the law as we know it. They attend to the various ways that physical pain and other kinds of suffering appear in law as well as the ways they are similar to, and distinguishable from, one another. These essays call on us to ask how various audiences understand the pain and death of others, how they make sense of both experienced vicariously, and how those audiences imagine what pain and death would mean if they were in the others' situation. Throughout this book law is regarded as a domain in which the meanings of pain and death are contested, and constituted in the contest, as well as an instrument for inflicting physical pain or for refusing its relief.

The first essay, by Karl Shoemaker, provides an overview of the way the idea of pain has figured in thinking about punishment since the eighteenth century. Historicizing and relativizing the construction of pain, he notes the rather dramatic shift away from what he calls "extravagant corporal and capital penalties" that has occurred during that period. Shoemaker argues that we should examine this "exiling of the deliberate infliction of physical pain" for what it can tell us about ourselves. He notes that other scholars have generally failed to examine how punishment is given meaning through its association with, or distance from, pain and how pain, at least in part, is constructed and given meaning by its association with punishment.

---

39. They do not treat pain and death as natural phenomena, but rather as social events that are acknowledged through grounded social practices. See David Morris, "About Suffering: Voice, Genre, and Moral Community," *Daedalus* 125 (1996): 40.

40. Veena Das, "Language and Body: Transactions in the Construction of Pain," *Daedalus* 125 (1996): 70.

In Shoemaker's view, crucial to the historical transformation of punishment has been a shift in prevailing views about the intelligibility and cultural significance of pain. Relying especially on readings of Dante and Hegel, he suggests that since the eighteenth century we have tended to presuppose pain as a motive for human action, as something to be externally imposed by political authority, and to treat it as a means to achieve social ends. In contrast, earlier understandings did not treat pain as a motive for action, but instead as derived from the relation of the human soul to the good. Pain was taken to be a sign of internal strife in the soul, and not necessarily an evil, but a constituent element of the human condition.

Shoemaker contends that transcendent understandings of pain's place in the medieval Christian world (Dante), or in the philosophical idealism of Hegel, give way to a view in which pain ceases to occupy an intelligible place in the world, a view given its clearest recent expression in Scarry's *Body in Pain*. "Pain," he says, "in crucial respects, has become unintelligible to us." Yet when pain appears in the practice of punishment it is nonetheless regarded as a necessary evil, one that "civilized" societies may use, albeit reluctantly, with that reluctance being taken as a mark of their civilization.

The next essay, by Austin Sarat, takes up the view that, in late modern society, pain is a necessary evil and tries to show how law legitimates itself through its "scrupulous" concern to minimize the pain of punishment. The particular focus of this argument is contemporary Supreme Court cases dealing with the constitutionality of methods of capital punishment—hanging, gas, electrocution, lethal injection. In these cases, we can see how pain is constructed in legal discourse as well as how it gives meaning to law itself.

One of the deep contradictions of state killing in the United States, Sarat argues, is that even as the death penalty responds to, and stirs up the passion to "do unto others . . . ," the recent history of execution is marked by recurrent efforts to find ever more "humane" technologies for taking life. How do we make sense of that fact? His contribution suggests that images and imaginings of pain play a key role. The movement from hanging to electrocution, from electrocution to the gas chamber, from gas to lethal injection, reads like someone's version of the triumph of progress, with each new technique enthusiastically embraced as the latest and best way to kill without imposing pain.

Indeed efforts to "read" pain have become central to the jurisprudence of death. There pain is assumed to be legible, if not fully intelligible, making its appearance as a series of signs on the body. As a result, courts can present themselves as able to insure that state killing imposes no more pain than is necessary to the accomplishment of that purpose.

Thus in most of the cases on the constitutionality of particular methods of execution the key question is "Do these methods kill painlessly?" Yet one might quite reasonably ask whether the state should be concerned about the suffering of those it puts to death. In addition, what does it tell us about the way law regards punishment that we seek to kill, but yet to kill gently? It is not, as some in the victims rights movement have argued, that we are moved by misplaced sympathy. The quest to kill painlessly, Sarat contends, is better understood as an act of grace, or better yet, as itself part of a strategy of legal legitimation in an era marked by ambivalence in its attitudes toward the place of pain in punishment.

In "What the Law Must Not Hear," Timothy Kaufman-Osborn examines the legal construction of pain and death as it takes shape in two court decisions dealing with different methods of capital punishment. The first, *Campbell v. Wood,* considered the question of pain inflicted by hanging; and the second, *Provenzano v. Moore,* considered the same issue with respect to electrocution. In part, his concern is with the rhetorical strategies employed by the dissenters in these cases in an effort to render pain palpably real and so bolster their claims about the cruelty of these two methods. More fundamentally, however, this essay reveals what Kaufman-Osborn claims to be the impoverished rhetoric of pain that is common to the defenders as well as the opponents of capital punishment in general and of these methods more particularly.

Following Elaine Scarry, one might, he argues, explain this impoverishment through reference to what she calls pain's essential incommunicability, that is, its stubborn resistance to linguistic expression. That claim, however, fails to take account of the fact that different languages can be more or less rich in their capacity to render pain articulate. Indeed, Kaufman-Osborn insists that, for political purposes, pain is in large measure a discursively constructed reality.

In making this case, he draws on the work of Sharon Marcus and others who have rejected the view that the pain caused by rape is a nondiscursive "brute fact." On the basis of her representation of rape as a scripted rhetorical reality, Marcus argues that the suffering inflicted

by this deed is a variable construction, that is, one that will be ampli-
fied, diminished, and/or refashioned depending on its mode of linguistic articulation. If Marcus is right, and if her argument can be
extended to the pain caused by capital punishment, then, Kaufman-
Osborn notes, it follows that an acknowledgment of pain's discursive
nature, combined with the development of a more nuanced vocabulary, may open up new ways of talking about, and so more effectively
opposing, the cruelty of capital punishment.

The development of such a vocabulary, as well as to effort to show
how law has come to rely on pain as a key to grounding of judgment,
are key components of Jennifer Culbert's "The Sacred Name of Pain:
The Role of Victim Impact Evidence in Death Penalty Sentencing Decisions." This essay continues the focus of *Pain, Death, and the Law* on
state killing as a particularly apt moment to assess the place of pain and
death in law as well as to examine their discursive construction in legal
decisions. Thus she examines several recent Supreme Court cases about
victim impact evidence in capital cases, cases in which the Court first
found the use of that evidence unconstitutional, but then overruled its
previous decisions. The reason for this reversal, Culbert contends, has
to do with the Court's recognition of a crisis of legal legitimacy associated with the fact that "those who would judge . . . are more or less condemned to the sincere but ethically banal and morally unsatisfactory
position that 'everything is relative.'"

Victim impact evidence liberates sentencing authorities in capital
cases from this situation, providing, as Culbert sees it, "a unique moral
power in a liberal, pluralist society." Reading the decisions on victim
impact evidence, Culbert suggests that the Court treats the pain of the
survivors as an absolute "in a society in which every other kind of
claim is subject to contestation, doubt, and criticism." Responding to
the pain of victims has become for law a "sacred name," namely an
ideal or principle in terms of which the good is defined by society.

In capital trials, expressions of pain are distinguished by the fact
that they are at once universal and particular. The circumstances that
give rise to pain as well as the suffering it engenders are, in Culbert's
view, always particular. Yet pain is also an experience with which
everyone is familiar. Courts give pain a meaning that connects the distinctiveness of individual experience with the "grounds for judgment
that people from different cultural backgrounds and all walks of life
share." Moreover, the experience of pain is precisely one that cannot be

refuted. "When survivors speak of their pain in court, what they say is rendered . . . more certain by their personal proximity to death . . . [since] death is the only shared certainty." Thus, like Sarat's interest in the role of pain in the legitimation of law, Culbert suggests that pain and death now play crucial roles in law, providing a key answer to the question "In the name of what or whom do we judge?"

The final contribution to this book moves away from capital punishment to examine the place of pain in cases on the right to die. Yet it recognizes that here, as in the law's treatment of state killing, these cases pivot, as Shai Lavi puts it, on the "right to die a painless death." While courts have not fully articulated such a right in either area, in the right-to-die cases, as in the cases on capital punishment discussed by Sarat and Kaufman-Osborn, pain plays a key role.

Lavi argues that physician-assisted suicide and other right-to-die claims emerge in response to particular constructions of the problem of pain. Initially courts thought about the right to die as a problem of ascertaining the will of the patient or his surrogates and determining that that expressed will was valid. More recently courts have turned away from the subjective wish of the patient, grounding their decisions on assessments of her objective condition. Thus as the passive withholding of medical treatment and its active withdrawal have become medically accepted means of relieving the pain of the dying patient, court's have relied on a rather crude calculus of pain. They measure it by its intensity and understand it primarily as a bodily sensation. They assume that life is worth living only if the balance of pleasure outweighs pain.

In this essay Lavi asks why this is the case. "How is it that the pain accompanying the dying process has become intolerable?" He demonstrates that the answer cannot be found in a simple translation of the principles of utility into legal language, since utilitarians like Bentham did not consider pain to be primarily a bodily sensation, but rather an "affective category, one relating to the emotions." Moreover, the answer to this question cannot be found in the fact that dying has become more painful, for, as Lavi explains, "the reverse is true." Thus it is not the physiology of pain that is crucial.

On the contrary, what Lavi calls the "perceived intensification of the pain of dying" is the result of particular moral, medical, and legal constructions. Like Kaufman-Osborn, Lavi explicitly takes issue with Scarry. Pain does not either escape or destroy language. It is known, through various, though particular, discourses. In the context of the right to die, and in the legal construction of pain in that context, medical discourses have a played key role. Pain, Lavi contends contra Culbert, is the consequence, not the ground, of these constructions. Pain then becomes a problem for law, whether in the right to die or in the death penalty, when and where it comes to be seen as senseless. In the eyes of the law, "Pain can be suffered only as long as it can be understood and justified."

It may be the distinctive business of law in the late modern era to both understand pain and death and to justify them. Yet, as the essays in *Pain, Death, and the Law* show, the appearance and construction of pain and death as facts of legal life are complex and contingent. The brute physicality of pain and death neither overwhelms law nor compels attention. Thus law attends to pain and death selectively, purposively, though never without contestation, making both visible in order to legitimate itself or provide grounds for its judgments. And, in its attendance to pain and death, law helps to construct their social meaning, providing a context in which neither is, if either could be, willed into exile. Both are treated as legible, if not wholly intelligible, conditions of the lives that we lead, one marking life's horizon, the other being a condition to which law may condemn us or from which it may help us make an escape. In the end, then, the essays collected here suggest that if we are to understand pain and death, we must turn to law, and that if we are to understand law, we must turn to pain and death.

The Problem of Pain
in Punishment:
Historical Perspectives

Karl Shoemaker

Within a relatively short period of years, beginning roughly in the latter portion of the eighteenth century, a wide range of corporal punishments employed throughout western Europe and the American
colonies gave way to less bloody penal methods. By the early nineteenth century, a multitude of different capital punishments, including
burning, hanging, exposure, and dismemberment, and an even broader
range of noncapital bodily punishments, such as maiming, branding,
dunking, and flogging, were replaced, with only a few exceptions, by
incarceration. This rather sudden and comprehensive shift from extravagant corporal and capital penalties toward incarceration was tethered
to a dramatic reduction in the amount of physical suffering experienced in punishment. No longer did punishment focus upon the dra-
maturgy of a condemned undergoing intense physical pain; now punishment operated without bloodletting, with minimized physical
suffering, and almost exclusively within the walls of a penitentiary.

This essay asks after the sense of this transformation. How are we
to understand this movement in which physical pain and suffering no
longer stand as explicitly intended and prominent elements of punishment? If, as modern scholarship suggests, punishment is intimately
bound up with cultural sensibilities, both reflecting and shaping our
understandings of ourselves and our world, then this swift and sure
exiling of the deliberate infliction of physical pain from punishment, a

movement to which we are heirs, must tell us something about ourselves.[1]

But what are we told about ourselves in this transformation? A
range of answers has been offered to the question of this decline in
painful punishments. One school of thought, argued forcefully by
Pieter Spierenburg, finds in this transformation a rise of humanitarian
sensibilities.[2] In the early modern period, the argument runs, a dominant mentality arose in the West that found the spectacle of pain and
suffering repulsive and that actively sought, as a moral imperative,
forms of punishment that did minimal violence to the body. Another
account, furthered by the cultural historian Thomas Haskell, ties the
abandonment of physically painful punishments to a broad range of
cultural transformations that culminated in a new "cognitive style" that
no longer accepted the lavish and promiscuous sufferings of the ancien
régime.[3] By this account, the same modes of causal thinking that gave
rise to capitalism and modern commercial exchange also enabled criticism and eventually abolition of corporal punishment on grounds that
at once encompassed self-interest and altruism. A still separate
account, made famous by Michel Foucault, finds not a humanitarian
sentiment, but a more refined configuration of authority in which
power is stamped more effectively on the soul than on the body.[4] Thus,
the infliction of pain fades from modern punishment, not because we
became more moral, but because authority received a greater return of
"epistemological dominance" when prison discipline replaced the gallows and the whipping post.

We shall have opportunity to examine these accounts further, but
the treatment of pain in each is striking. While each notes the historical
diminishment of the physical pain inflicted in modern punishment, the
significance of pain itself, the manner in which pain is understood as a
facet of punishment, seems to recede from view. A movement is identi-

---

1. David Garland, *Punishment and Modern Society: A Study in Modern Social Thought*
(Chicago: University of Chicago Press, 1994), 249–92.

2. Pieter Spierenburg, *The Spectacle of Suffering: Executions and the Evolution of Repres-
sion* (Cambridge: Cambridge University Press, 1984); Spierenburg, "The Body and the
State: Early Modern Europe," in *The Oxford History of the Prison: The Practice of Punishment
in Western Society,* ed. Norval Morris and David J. Rothman (New York: Oxford University Press, 1985), 44–70.

3. Thomas L. Haskell, "Capitalism and the Origins of the Humanitarian Sensibility," *American Historical Review* 90 (1985): 339–61 (part 1), 547–66 (part 2).

4. Michel Foucault, *Discipline and Punish,* trans. Alan Sheridan (New York: Vintage,
1977).

fied in each of these works in which physically painful punishments become socially unacceptable, or in conflict with capitalist values, or less useful to authority, but the substance of these asserted transformations is less clear. One asks: What were the conditions of thought that previously had allowed pain to play such a central role in punishment? Likewise, what conditions of thought so rapidly made painful forms of punishment unacceptable relics of the past? Can it be that the intelligibility of pain itself has transformed? Could it be that a central driving force behind the transformation in modern penal modes has been bound up with a shift in our understanding of pain itself?

In important respects, these questions have gone unasked in the scholarly treatment of modern penal transformations. Nonetheless, these questions suggest something very important about our understanding of the place of pain in punishment. Part 1 of this essay is devoted to sharpening the question of the significance of pain in punishment from within the leading sociological and historical accounts of the rise of the prison and the demise of older, more painful, punishments.

Part 2 is dedicated to uncovering what is said about the place of pain in punishment within our historical tradition. Given that premodern punishments were often lavishly and famously painful, what conditions of thought, what understandings of the world, made such practices intelligible and seemingly proper ways to punish? Through a historical lens, two hallmark articulations of the place of pain in punishment, those of Dante and Hegel, will be examined and placed alongside certain modern understandings. Despite the philosophical and historical distance that separates Dante from Hegel, the similarities and common foundations in their understandings of pain's place in punishment put them together on the other side of a great divide separating our thinking from theirs. Hence, we will gain, if only in broad outlines, the sense of an important transformation in our own thinking on pain in punishment. To anticipate and to put the matter too schematically: the understandings of pain in punishment that come to prevail in the eighteenth and nineteenth centuries, and that have taken hold until today, tend to presuppose pain as (1) a motive for human action; (2) something to be externally imposed by authority; and (3) a necessary, though perhaps evil, means to achieve social ends. In contrast, earlier understandings contemplated the feeling of pain in punishment as (1) not a motive for action, but derived from the relation of the human soul to the good; (2) thus, primarily an internal strife of the soul, rather than externally imposed; and (3) not necessarily an evil, but a constituent element of the human condition.

Part 3, the final part of this essay, revisits the modern transformation of punishment by looking to the arguments of eighteenth- and nineteenth-century penal reformers in order to flesh out this intellectual transformation. For it is here, in these widespread penal transformations, that the modern understanding of pain and its relationship with punishment takes concrete form and occasions such a remarkable breach with past thinking. By looking at selected writings on punishment that emerge in the eighteenth and nineteenth centuries, and in particular at the apologies for penitentiaries, we see a movement in which pain ceases to occupy an intelligible place in the world. Here, the transcendent understandings of pain's place in the medieval Christian world, or the philosophical system of Hegel's idealism, give way to understandings of punishment that see pain as essentially evil, but nevertheless useful in correcting and disciplining wrongdoers. Ironically, in some respects, the earliest proponents of the penitentiary retain in their understandings the older structure of Christian penance, but place the conditions for that penance decisively in human hands. Thus, pain now takes its place as a prompting, employed by authority to achieve particular ends, but no longer bestowing (indeed, no longer able to bestow) a meaning upon the world, as it had in earlier understandings.

The movement of thought that will emerge in the rise of the penitentiary and the demise of corporal punishments, this essay argues, underlies the whole of modern Western thinking concerning punishment. Indeed, this transformation implicates much more than the policies and programs implemented to address criminality in a manner consistent with our present values (be those values efficiency, humaneness, deterrence, prevention, rehabilitation, etc., or some combination thereof). Rather, at bottom, the path of modern penal practices and their posture toward bodily suffering and pain reveal a change in our understandings of ourselves and the place we hold in this world. No longer an emblem of man's finitude to be embraced and no longer concomitant with man's striving in relation to the divine, pain stands for us as a self-evident evil, calling, it seems, for its own eradication from all modes of our existence. In short, and to anticipate the argument: Pain itself, in crucial respects, has become unintelligible to us. It is clear that penal forms that once bespoke a clear vision of man's place in the world, both in relation to others as well as to the divine, would amount to senseless brutality today. But perhaps punishment itself, notwithstanding its relative lack of corporal pain, can be nothing but brutality for us today. It remains for us to attempt to glean the significance of this transformation of the place of pain in punishment. Lauding it, just as lamenting it, will mean little until we see more clearly how we come to stand in the place we do today.

I

Among recent historical treatments of the early modern transformations in penal modes, Pieter Spierenburg takes most seriously the claim that those penal reformers who objected to painful forms of traditional punishments were driven by a genuine humanitarian sentiment. The history of penal evolution in the early modern and modern West, according to Spierenburg, is largely the story of a "growing sensitivity to violence and an aversion to physical suffering."[5] Spierenburg's story begins in the late Middle Ages, where we find a prevailing sensibility that easily accepts "the open infliction of pain" and unashamed enjoyment in watching others suffer.[6] Punishment, too, in this age sometimes took on gruesome forms. By the early modern period, however, many of the older forms of punishment were falling out of use, and a groundswell of opposition to the bloody excesses of certain penal forms was apparent. A transformation occurred in which punishment grew less painful and perhaps less cruel. To be sure, Spierenburg is alert to the insufficiency of describing "the evolution of criminal justice in simple terms, such as a gradual progress away from cruelty."[7] Still, he does not want the language of humanitarian reformers to be dismissed.

Rather, he celebrates the Enlightenment era reformers as motivated by a genuine benevolence, but also as sharing a mentality that actively shaped and determined the socially acceptable forms of punishment. Spierenburg attempts to explore the role that this changing mentality played in the development of the modern state and its mech-

---

5. Spierenburg, "Body and State," 47.
6. Spierenburg, *The Spectacle of Suffering,* 54.
7. Spierenburg, "Body and State," 47.

anisms of punishment. Spierenburg asserts that changing sensibilities and attitudes serve as a restraining and determining link between developing states and penal measures.[8] As David Garland captures Spierenburg's point: "To the extent that punishment implies . . . the infliction of pain and suffering, its development will be affected by the ways in which prevailing sensibilities differentiate between permissible and impermissible forms of violence, and by cultural attitudes towards the sight of pain."[9] Thus, Spierenburg's project locates the evolution of less painful punishments in a cultural attitude, or mentality, that restrains the acceptable forms in which state authority can punish.

Seen this way, Spierenburg's work on punishment is situated within the wider framework of Norbert Elias's work on the civilizing process. As Elias tells us of medieval life generally, and not in the specific context of punishment, "the pleasure in killing and torturing others was great, and it was a socially permitted pleasure."[10] Gradually, explains Elias, and beginning with the higher social strata, the delight in cruelty became restrained, privatized, and in important respects, suppressed. With the gradual emergence of territorial principalities, and the demobilization of the knightly warrior ethic so prominent in the earlier period, so the argument runs, punishment too became less imbued with cruelty, more private, and more austere. Thus, within a broad movement toward an increasingly civilized society, modes of punishment kept pace with wider cultural sensibilities.

Standard scholarly accounts criticize Elias's or Spierenburg's apologies for the humanitarian impulse in such cultural transformations on the ground that they naively accept the rhetoric of Enlightenment reformers without adequately accounting for other interests. The history of the modern West, say these critics, is not the story of an unfaltering progress toward morality, and humanitarian sentiments often mask less altruistic goals. Without engaging directly with the merits of these critiques, we can make a more immediate observation: however accepting Spierenburg is of the humanitarian narrative, little concerning the cultural significance of pain, and its intelligibility in the prac-

---

8. Spierenburg, *The Spectacle of Suffering*, 12, 201; Garland, *Punishment and Modern Society*, 229.

9. Garland, *Punishment and Modern Society*, 214.

10. Norbert Elias, *The Civilizing Process*, trans. Edmund Jephcott (1939; Oxford: Oxford University Press, 1978), 2:194 (published in the United States under the title *Power and Civility*).

tices of the medieval world, can be gleaned from his account. As a descriptive matter, we can characterize one aspect of this transformation as follows: Pain, once openly inflicted and suffered, becomes gradually suppressed; not only removed from public sight but no longer an unabashed pleasure. Still, the reasons why pain became unacceptable to widely held sensibilities are difficult to pin down in Spierenburg's account.

For one thing, despite Spierenburg's careful attention to cultural mentalities, the medieval penal practices that casually or enthusiastically embraced the infliction of pain, and that stand in stark opposition to the austere discipline of the modern era, are not fleshed out a great deal. Aside from an unashamed enjoyment in the festival of cruelty, little is said about the wider context within which medieval sensibilities concerning punishment and pain were situated. A compelling account is given in which gradual but certain progress from the medieval attitudes toward more civilized sensibilities marks the entirety of the West. Yet the discussion of the attitudes toward pain and suffering proceeds without exploring the conditions of thought that allowed for a pleasure in cruelty or an acceptance of bloody dismemberment in punishment. Any affirmative sense possessed by the older punishments, the understanding of the world upon which they rested (and which perhaps they granted), seems buried beneath Spierenburg's commitment to locating the rise of a humanitarian sensibility. We will examine the grounds upon which pain might have been understood in the Middle Ages below. But, in the end, Spierenburg leaves us saying merely that whatever physically painful punishment formerly signified as a cultural and perhaps even theological matter, moral sensibilities transformed in such a way that the "spectacle of suffering" was no longer acceptable.

If Spierenburg enthusiastically accepts the humanitarian foundations of modern punishment as an explanation for the decline in its painfulness, Thomas Haskell takes a more cautious approach. Haskell attempts to carve out an honored place for the "courage" and "commendable changes" of humanitarian reform while allowing that less altruistic interests of reformers were served as well.[11] The explanation for the movement toward seemingly less cruel forms of punishment, he suggests, may be more complicated than Spierenburg allows. Haskell endeavors to overcome the simplistic but traditional tension that, in

---

11. Haskell, "Capitalism and Humanitarian Sensibility," 339, 340.

seeking to explain various transformations in modern social practices, seems to force a choice between a so-called humanitarian sentiment and less philanthropic bourgeois economic interests.[12] In so doing, Haskell does not give sustained attention to transformations in penal modes, but he does provide a framework within which the decreasing severity of punishments in the modern era might be explained.[13]

For Haskell, the humanitarian narrative of the Enlightenment era commentators must be understood against the backdrop of the capitalism that emerges at the dawn of the modern era. What grounded both marketplace success and the new humanitarian mentality of the Enlightenment era, argues Haskell, were "altered perceptions of causation in human affairs."[14] The foundation upon which market discipline and humanitarian sensibilities rested was both the power to keep promises and a more refined ability to foresee consequences. It is this "new cognitive style," characterized in large part by an interplay between faith in the effectiveness of human action and a related extension of responsibility, that allows for a belief in the ability to locate the causes of human suffering and to ameliorate them.[15] Thus, as Haskell would have it, a new mode of thought arose in which humanitarian impulses fit comfortably beside the causal thinking that grounded the self-interested forms of capitalism. Hence, if, in accord with Spierenburg, painful forms of punishment were coming into increasing tension with Enlightenment sensibilities, Haskell suggests that this tension was driven by a new understanding of causation in the world. No longer content to passively accept the older traditions of excruciating penal sentences, Enlightenment reformers came to understand social practices, as well as their anticipated consequences, as within their power to change.

This new "cognitive style," according to Haskell, had a wider purchase than penal forms alone. This new mode of thinking influenced a wide range of social practices, from the movement to abolish slavery to

---

12. Haskell, "Capitalism and Humanitarian Sensibility," 340. See also George Fisher, "The Birth of the Prison Retold," *Yale Law Journal* 104 (1995): 1237. Fisher's own explanation for the rise of the prison over older forms of punishment looks to the arguments made by contemporary writers regarding the punishment of young wrongdoers and finds there the expansion of these reformative principles extended over a broader class of convicts.

13. Haskell, "Capitalism and Humanitarian Sensibility," 342.

14. Ibid.

15. Haskell, "Capitalism and Humanitarian Sensibility," 547, 551.

transformations in contract law doctrine. And whether the rhetoric surrounding the reformers was largely what we would call humanitarian, as with slavery, or more concerned with furthering commercial exchange, as was the case with contract law, Haskell understands both as resting on a common mode of thinking.

When this new cognitive style turned toward punishment, the focus came to be upon the long-term effects of punishment, the ability to deter others, and to reduce crime. At the same time, the willingness in the older punishments to inflict excessive suffering gave way to both an aversion to this pain and a conviction that more moderate punishment actually might be more effective in achieving deterrence and reduced criminality. Thus, supplementing Spierenburg, we can account for the mode of thinking that perhaps underlay the changing sensibilities toward suffering that have marked punishment since the Enlightenment period. Following Haskell, we can now suggest that pain comes to be understood as something that needs to be (and can be) planned and measured if punishment is to be effective and rational.[16]

Still, the grounds for the intelligibility of the pain inflicted in the premodern penal forms remain, in this account, obscure. Perhaps, then, the sanguinary punishments of the ancien régime can be accounted for as a resigned comportment toward suffering. Without the Enlightenment ambition for reforms, one might argue, the older modes of punishment were passively accepted and remained in their customary, bloody form. The pain of these older corporal punishments would seem, in retrospect, to lie beyond the power of human reason and effectiveness to prevent until the onset of the "cognitive style" of the Enlightenment. New understandings of human agency brought pain within the ambit of things a humane and rational legislator could control and plan. If with Spierenburg we could identify a transformation in sensibilities but say little about its essence, with Haskell we can see that

---

16. Through a slightly different lens, Thomas Laqueur offers support for Haskell's thesis as it pertains to the human body and pain. See "Bodies, Details, and the Humanitarian Narrative," in *The New Cultural History: Essays,* ed. Lynn Hunt (Berkeley and Los Angeles: University of California Press, 1989). Laqueur argues that Enlightenment thinking comes to see the body as the locus of pain and to discuss the amelioration of that pain through the lineaments of causality and human agency. This focus upon the body and remote causation is made explicit in Laqueur's discussion of the detailed manner in which documents such as autopsy reports, as well as novels, came to be written. This suggests that the primacy of the humanitarian project regarding the alleviation of pain and suffering gained a foothold once causal thinking and consequential planning had taken root.

a new way of thinking marks the emergence of the modern world. Man's new found understanding of the world around him could now also be turned toward the amelioration of human suffering.

Perhaps the most famous account of modern penal transformations has been presented by Michel Foucault in *Discipline and Punish.* There, Foucault rejects in forceful terms the thesis that penal history is marked first and foremost by heightened moral attitudes and sensibilities that prompted a move from less humane to more humane forms of punishment. Foucault, instead, places penal history primarily within the dynamics of social power, knowledge, and the structures of the state. The move away from the scaffold and public corporal punishments and toward incarceration is driven, he argues, by an urge to make punishment better, more efficient and more effective, in terms of social control, not by an emergent moral sensibility.

For one thing, Foucault turns the sentiment of humanitarian reform on its head. After reciting some representative eighteenth-century humanitarian expressions concerning the need for moderation in punishment, Foucault states: "The body, the imagination, pain, the heart to be respected are not, in effect, those of the criminal that is to be punished, but those men who, having subscribed to the pact, have the right of exercising against him the power of assembly."[17] What humanitarian language veils, says Foucault, is that what "has to be arranged and calculated are the return effects of punishment on the punishing authority and the power that it claims to exercise."[18] Even more directly, Foucault states: "If the law must now treat in a 'humane' way . . . , it is not on account of some profound humanity that the criminal conceals within him, but because of a necessary regulation of the effects of power."[19]

In Foucault's framework then, if punishment became less painful to the physical body, it was because authority received a greater return by focusing its energies on discipline and control than on merely scrawling its power on individual bodies. In some ways the dependence of authority upon the power sustained through punishment remains a constant historical factor for Foucault. While writers such as Spierenburg see a transformation in sensibilities that translates directly into penal reforms, Foucault sees the move away from the ancien

---

17. Foucault, *Discipline and Punish,* 91.
18. Ibid.
19. Ibid., 92.

régime as undergirded by some of the same implied power-knowledge dynamics as the ancien régime itself.

In this light, Foucault's account begins to characterize the meaning which pain may have possessed in the older, more bloody forms of punishment. The older practices of torture and public punishments themselves, argues Foucault, "belong to a political technology of the body," as much as the later discipline of the prison would.[20] In the older punishments, this political technology directed itself toward the very body of the condemned. Echoing an aspect of Nietzschean thought, Foucault sees the punishments of the ancien régime as a ritual display of strength similar to victory over an enemy in warfare.[21] The significance of the brutality of the ancien régime, he argued, was grounded in a reaffirmation of power by the sovereign. The body of the condemned became the material that the sovereign reshaped and even annihilated in the public spectacle. Although there eventually occurs a decline in public corporal punishment, much of the register of power-knowledge remains for Foucault. Rather than inscripting signs of power on the body of the condemned, authorities began "gaining access to the soul," where more effective change could be wrought.[22] As Garland captures Foucault's theme, "Prison seizes the body of the inmate," but now the concern is with "exercising it, training it, organizing its time and movement in order ultimately to transform the soul."[23]

Thus, for Foucault, pain is, and perhaps has always been, an accompaniment to punishment, but not its most necessary feature. If older punishments were extremely painful and directed at the body, the newer penalties used the body only "as an instrument or intermediary."[24] If the prison also implied pain, though of a more psychological sort, it was a by-product of the disciplinary structure imposed by authorities. Echoing Durkheim, Foucault writes, "Physical pain, the pain of the body itself, is no longer the constituent element of the penalty."[25] Because pain itself, for Foucault, is not understood as an

---

20. Ibid., 30.

21. Frederick Nietzsche, *The Genealogy of Morals,* trans. Walter Kaufman (New York: Vintage Books, 1967), 213; Foucault, *Discipline and Punish,* 57.

22. Garland, *Punishment and Modern Society,* 143.

23. Ibid.

24. Foucault, *Discipline and Punish,* 11.

25. Ibid. See, e.g., Émile Durkheim, *Moral Education,* trans. Everett K. Wilson and Herman Schnurer (New York: Free Press, 1973), 182; as well as Garland's discussion in chapter 2 of *Punishment and Modern Society.*

essential feature of punishment, pain's disappearance from modern punishment requires no focused explanation. Punishment, understood as a "mechanism[] of power that frame[s] the everyday lives of individuals,"[26] need not be painful to render to authority that which it seeks—the epistemological dominance of its subjects. For Foucault, the transformation in modern punishment is only incidentally marked by a new understanding of pain. The crucial point, as he sees it, revolves not around the pain inflicted upon the body, but on the power exercised upon the soul. But even so, pain appears to be thought only as a force moderated to achieve certain effects.

Through these three accounts of the modern history of punishment we can identify unifying themes concerning the significance of the pain experienced in punishment. Through the lens of humanitarian sensibilities, we can see that the modern age is marked by an aversion to the pain and suffering that condemned once underwent as a matter of course. The essence of this transformation may be murky, but it is undeniable that punishments became less public and inflicted less direct physical suffering. Further, through the work of Haskell, we can identify a transformation of "cognitive style" in which calculative thinking not only secured market discipline but allowed for a call to ameliorative action in regard to penal forms as a moral imperative. This allowed a transition that brought the pain inflicted in punishment within the power of reformers, or the authorities, to regulate and moderate. In turn, this regulation and moderation of punishment's painfulness was carried out in the light of rational goals, namely, deterrence and prevention (or perhaps, for Foucault, discipline and surveillance).

But through all this, certain central questions regarding the way pain's place in punishment has been historically understood remain. On what grounds could pain have once been such an integral part of punishment? On what grounds, precisely, could Enlightenment reformers make pain into a nonessential aspect of punishment? That is, on what grounds could an "evolving mentality," or a "new cognitive style," or a new understanding of epistemological dominance push pain to the periphery of punishment—remaining perhaps as a threat but no longer essential?

As we shall see, it may not be completely accurate to say that pain itself has been pushed to the periphery of punishment, but rather that

---

26. Foucault, *Discipline and Punish,* 77.

our understanding of punishment's pain has become so reflexive, so unquestioned, that we do not see the difficulties. But as we seek after the understanding of pain in punishment that perhaps still grounds modern punishment, even as modern punishment is explicitly painful only at the margins, we will also need to ascertain the affirmative sense which pain has held within punishment in the Western tradition.

II

Modern writers have not neglected the question of pain altogether. Two writers may serve as representative of the modern questioning after pain's place in punishment. Nils Christie, a contemporary writer who urges that we confront pain as a "commodity" delivered by the state, advocates for alternatives to any sort of pain in punishment, including the sort suffered in well-functioning incarceral institutions, by the removal of the apparatus of crime control from the modern state.[27] Far removed from Christie's project, Graeme Newman has argued that "acute corporal punishment should be introduced to fill the gap between the severe punishment of prison and the non-punish-ment of probation."[28] Newman's project stems from the conviction that modern criminal justice is submerged in abysmal failure and can be rectified if we remember what our ancestors appear to have known: "Punishment must, above all else, be painful."[29] To this end, Newman urges "electric shock because it can be scientifically controlled and cal-ibrated."[30]

While it should be emphasized how little this essay purports to enter the policy debate between Christie and Newman, it is striking to consider certain of their shared premises. Namely, pain is an efficient, likely the most efficient, way for authority to control behavior; it is pri-marily a physical experience of something externally imposed; and it is a "commodity" that can be "scientifically controlled and calibrated." The common ground of the thinking of these two seemingly opposed writers only serves to strengthen the central theme of this essay—that our historical understanding of pain's meaning in punishment has

---

27. Nils Christie, *Limits to Pain* (New York: Columbia University Press, 1981), 1–26.
28. Graeme Newman, *Just and Painful: A Case for the Corporal Punishment of Criminals* (New York: Macmillan, 1983), 139.
29. Ibid., 6.
30. Ibid., 139.

undergone a remarkable transformation. Indeed, these assumptions concerning the nature of pain in punishment seem also to be threaded throughout the historical and sociological accounts examined above.

But there are other ways in which punishment's pain has been understood in our intellectual tradition. This section is concerned with exploring the senses in which pain was understood in the period preceding the Enlightenment movement away from corporal punishments. Perhaps the emblematic account of late-medieval conceptions of punishment is found in Dante's *Divine Comedy.* Dante's work is not, of course, concerned with justifying the forms of punishment employed in his age, or for that matter doctrines of divine punishment. Rather, Dante's work holds "forth the abstractions of scholastic thinking" in bodily form, "turning them to shapes and giving them a local habitation and name."[31] Dante's thinking is central here because "his imagination work[ed] habitually within [the] system . . . of theology and cosmology of the Middle Ages."[32] Thus, the understanding of pain and punishment that resides in Dante's thought will provide a backdrop against which we can understand the attitude toward punishment in modernity.

Nor is it supposed that Dante's presuppositions reflect everyday practice in the medieval world. For while it is true that a wide range of explicitly painful punishments were known and employed in the Middle Ages, it is also true that medieval criminal law often employed these punishments in only very particular circumstances. It must be remembered that many procedural and customary impediments to corporal and capital punishments were available throughout the legal traditions of the West. Procedural delays at trial were relatively easy to obtain. Further, many forms of pardon, including sanctuary and the benefit of clergy, as well as royal pardons, were not infrequently obtained. Moreover, the Roman church had a long-standing opposition to any punishment that drew blood, and thus in principle secular courts were left to exact such sanctions where the church's jurisdiction did not reach or, in special cases, where a condemned was handed over to the secular arm. Still, if an accused did find himself on the gallows, or on some other apparatus of punishment, he was likely to undergo

---

31. *The Divine Comedy of Dante Alighieri,* trans. John D. Sinclair (New York: Oxford University Press, 1961), 11.

32. Ibid., 10.

intense physical suffering. We turn to Dante, then, for insights into the medieval world's understanding of this suffering.

It is a commonplace that *The Divine Comedy* presents punishment as a painful undertaking. The gradation of Hell's rings, in which torments become more loathsome and the register of pain often grows more intense with each descending level, is legendary. In Hell, wrongdoers, understood by Dante as sinners, are subjected to punishments meant to reflect some essential feature of their wrong. Gluttons are pelted with foul rain and clawed by "Cerberus, the great worm."[33] In one case, the soul of a suicide is given form as a tree, upon whose branches its corpse shall be made to hang shamefully after the Last Judgment as a tribute to the self-inflicted violence.[34] In the farthest depths of Hell, Brutus, Cassius, and Judas are chewed upon by the jaws of Satan himself.[35] Nearby, "certain of the treacherous, wholly encased in ice, lose the pleasure even of a vicious society."[36]

Purgatory, too, is a place full of pain. Dante comments that not a man "walks on earth today . . . so hard that he would not have been pierced with pity" at what he saw there.[37] Each penitent in Purgatory must pass through an excruciatingly painful wall of fire on the terrace of lust, stagger under heavy loads on the terrace of pride, and fast while set before great feasts on the terrace of gluttony. With the significant exception of Purgatory's noneternal duration—those in Purgatory are, after all, gradually moving closer to paradise—it appears to be comprised of torments along the same design as Hell's.

Most significantly, though, pain is featured as a prominent element of punishment in both Hell and Purgatory. But what first must be seen here is how pain itself was understood in medieval traditions of thought. Medieval theologians had not neglected the question of pain. Indeed, it presented a particular challenge, for some form of the following question was always lurking: How can pain exist in a world created by an absolutely good God? The answer arrived at may seem strange at first. For Thomas Aquinas, whom Dante followed closely on

---

33. *Inferno*, canto vi, l. 22.
34. *Inferno*, canto xiii, ll. 105–7.
35. *Inferno*, canto xxxiv, ll. 55–57.
36. Michael Smith, "Punishment in *The Divine Comedy*," *Cumberland Law Review* 25 (1995): 533, 536. This discussion of Dante relies heavily upon the work of Smith.
37. *Purgatorio*, canto xiii, ll. 52–56.

this point, pain originated, not in the body, but first in the soul's desiring and striving for the good.[38] Indeed, Aquinas himself closely followed Augustine's thought on pain. As Augustine had written: "If,
however, we consider the matter more diligently, pain, which is said
[to be] of the body, pertains far more to the soul."[39] In the medieval
Christian understanding, pain is always concomitant with the human
will for the good. Because humans are limited, their desires are susceptible to the pain of being denied. Therefore, even the desire and pursuit
of the good is accompanied by pain, for it is a pursuit that cannot, given
man's finitude, be consummated. Moreover, although human desire
strives for the good, it happens that sometimes humans are deceived
and turned toward what is evil rather than good. It remains the case,
though, that whether the striving is for a real good or only an apparent
one, pain is an attribute of the desiring. In this way, all pain is at least
partly good. As Aquinas and Dante would have it, if the desire for a
merely apparent good, that is, an evil, is thwarted, good results. If, on
the other hand, desire for a real good is thwarted, it remains the case
that the love of that good, a condition of pain, is itself still good. Further, it should be noted that painful punishments are not presented by
Aquinas or Dante as a motive for conformity with the law. Rather, pain
encompasses all human action, whether directed at good or evil.
Indeed, insofar as one obeys the law only from a fear of punishment,
one betrays a certain baseness in the soul.[40] But in any event, the
thought of pain as a prompting for action is always derivative, for
Aquinas, from the pain that accompanies a deeper condition of the
soul.

From this standpoint, Dante would understand the pain suffered
by those in Hell in a manner completely different from the pain suffered by those in Purgatory. Strikingly, for Dante, the damned in Hell
do not know the true nature of their sufferings. While it appears to

---

38. On this point, see the recent historical essay by Esther Cohen, "The Animated
Body in Pain," *American Historical Review* (February 2000): 36–68, at 46 where the priority
of spiritual pain for Aquinas is discussed. She writes further: "Even the rare autobiogra-
phies we possess [from the medieval period] dwell far more on mental than physical
anguish" (37). And again she writes, "All major late medieval discourses on pain—in theology, medicine, and law—view 'physical' pain as a function of the soul" (42).

39. "Si autem consideremus diligentius, dolor, qui dicitur corporis, magis ad ani-
mam pertinet," *De civitate dei*, book 21, cap. 3, ed. Bernard Dombart and Alphonse Kalb
(Turnhout: 1955) in *Corpus Chistianorum Series Latina*. (Translation is my own.)

40. Aquinas, *The Treatise on Law: Being Summa Theologiae*, I–II, QQ. 90–97; trans. R. J.
Henle (Notre Dame: University of Notre Dame Press, 1993), 277.

them that they are being held captive and subjected to enormous suffering, in truth, their own desire holds them there. The damned persist in their desire for apparent rather than real goods. They simply have not, thinks Dante, resolved to seek the highest good and thus, they commit themselves to eternal pain in the endless thwarting of their desire. In the final analysis, it may be that Dante did not believe that those in Hell are totally deprived of the good. Rather, Hell "is as good as it can be for souls who are not committed to the good."[41] Nonetheless, the pain of their division, which seeks always chimera rather than the actual, is intense indeed. But it is precisely this division, furthered by their persistence in their crimes, that grounds the suffering of the Hell-bound. By Dante's understanding, the monsters in Hell that appear to agents of pain are only so in a derivative sense. The division in the will of the offender is the true source of his pain.

On the other hand, as Dante sees it, those in Purgatory seek God as their highest desire. Because the penitents' former sinful dispositions still beset them in Purgatory, their desire for God is still somewhat thwarted and must be gradually and slowly purified. It is this thwarting of desire that is the true source of their pain. But because this grief is experienced as a condition of seeking the true good, "the penitents know that for the sinful, the pains are a concomitant of the truly good."[42] Thus, it only appears as though their pains are applied by tortures from without. Rather, their true pain springs from their own desiring. This is how it can be that those in Purgatory are joyful toward their sufferings.[43] They see the truth of their pain, and its role in their redemption, and they seek it. Their pain indicates that they are shedding their sinful desires and moving closer to Paradise. The damned, who remain blind to the true good, remain forever in their pain.

Pain for Dante, as well as Aquinas, is always a part of punishment. Yet it is pain's spiritual aspect, the thwarting of the soul's desire, not its bodily aspect, that takes precedence. Further, Dante held, the pain experienced in punishment is capable of being experienced in radically opposite ways. The penitent are joyful in their pain, for they know what lies beyond. The damned, because they do not truly know what is good, languish in their pains. But in neither Hell nor Purgatory is pain applied to prompt action or to extract revenge. Rather, pain, always as

---

41. See, Smith, "Punishment in *The Divine Comedy*," 575.
42. Ibid., 567.
43. *Purgatorio*, canto xxvi, ll. 13–15.

a feature of frustrated desire, belongs to the structure of the soul and is not external to it. It follows also for Dante that pain, as an attribute of human desire, is not susceptible to quantification or application in a measured way. Moreover, bodily pain is always secondary and incidental to the spiritual division of the soul.[44]

It may be that Dante's thought regarding punishment, so thoroughly stamped as it was with teachings of the medieval church, has only faint relation with Western thinking on such matters since the Enlightenment. Further, as a poem, it may be that *The Divine Comedy* has nothing to say about mundane punishments. It is significant, though, that Dante, within the conditions of thought of his day, was able to present an understanding of punishment that gives pain a clear sense and an important place as a redemptive element within his world.

There is reason to think, however, that crucial aspects of Dante's thought are not dependent wholly upon the medieval scholasticism within which his thought moved. We turn now to Hegel, in order to see how the question of pain in punishment is carried out even after an explicit breach had occurred between philosophy and the dogma of the medieval church.

Modern writers on theoretical justifications of punishment have not neglected the writings of Hegel on law.[45] In standard scholarship, Hegel is put forward as an apologist for a "right to be punished."[46] As Hegel plainly states: "The hurt which befalls the criminal is . . . an embodiment of his freedom and his right."[47] But, as in Dante, this assertion regarding punishment can only be understood after Hegel's understanding of the nature of the pain that an offender undergoes is

---

44. Compare Elaine Scarry, *The Body in Pain: The Making and Unmaking of the World* (New York: Oxford University Press, 1985), 11, where the priority of these two types of pain is reversed on the grounds that psychological pain is said to have a referential content, while bodily pain does not.

45. See, e.g., Markus Dirk Dubber, "The Right to Be Punished: Autonomy and Its Demise in Modern Penal Thought," *Law and History Review* 16 (1998): 113; Matthew A. Pauley, "The Jurisprudence of Crime and Punishment from Plato to Hegel," *American Journal of Jurisprudence* 39 (1994): 97.

46. "The more daring among punishment apologists of the time went so far as to argue that the offender not only had consented to his punishment, but that he had the right to be punished" (Dubber, "Right to Be Punished," 115). This is said to follow for Hegel, as well as Kant, from their understanding of the nature of human freedom.

47. G. W. F. Hegel, *The Philosophy of Right,* trans. T. M. Knox (New York: Oxford University Press, 1967), sec. 100, p. 70.

explained. In Hegel, punishment itself is understood against the backdrop of a particular articulation of the pain. Hegel understands pain as the inner distress of a human soul. "Though its disclosure to man first occurs in the immediacy of sensibility," pain is not to be understood as a bodily sensation within Hegel's thought.[48] Pain is first felt by the natural body, but it is only known when one understands oneself to be a divided being, driven by longings that will never be fulfilled. As Hegel explains, the divided will, and thus pain, is always already implied in the will that would set itself against the law.

Indeed, this aspect of Hegel's thought is similar to Dante's. Recall that Dante saw those in Hell as misunderstanding the nature of their pains. Rather than seeing and desiring the highest good, the damned understood themselves as objects of punishment, receiving their pain from without. Thinking of punishment as consisting of a pain imposed from without by an "adverse power," says Hegel, is to understand punishment in a one-sided way, missing its transcendent significance.

In Hegel's thinking, the pain of punishment is properly understood as the will divided against itself by virtue of having attempted violence against the law. It is only through the pain of this division that the wrongdoer comes to see the wrongness of his deed. The crushing pain of punishment, then, also serves to reveal what is right; indeed, what is absolutely good. Only when this pain reaches its most desperate heights, and the will of the wrongdoer its point of lowest despair, does the wrongdoer see the unreality of his selfish existence apart from the absolute and come to know truth.[49]

For Hegel, this moment of the most crushing despair in the pain of punishment holds the significance of the pain in punishment. For pain leads the way to despair, and through that necessary course, shows the way to the redemption of the wrong. "In the moment of its completion, despair ceases to be despair, and the law of pain is fulfilled in the sanctification of pain, which is called sanction proper."[50] In the end, pain holds the promise of showing the way to the release of the innermost discord within the self.

In some ways, Hegel's thought, which speaks not in the language

48. Philippe Nonet, "Sanction," *Cumberland Law Review* 25 (1995): 516. The discussion of Hegel in this essay is heavily indebted to Nonet's work on Hegel and sanction.
49. Ibid.
50. Ibid., 519.

of religious doctrine but in the language of systematic philosophy, is more alien to us than Dante's. Nonetheless, we now have these small glimpses into possible ways to understand the pain experienced in punishment. First, for both Dante and Hegel, the physical manifestation of suffering is always derivative from the more fundamental pain of a self divided by a thwarted will, caught always between desire for the good and its fulfillment. That which the self desires, and therefore the mainspring of human action, is the good, or for Hegel, absolute knowledge. Further, the pain of punishment is not anything externally imposed. For these thinkers, whether the apparent minister of punishment be monstrous creatures in Hell or a judge in this world, the true significance of pain is internal to the offender. Moreover, for both Dante and Hegel, the pain experienced by the condemned ultimately allows him access to the transcendent. But in both cases, pain is world-bestowing, freeing man from his mundane and transitory existence.[51]

It is clear that when we examine both Dante and Hegel on the meaning of punishment we are far removed from the way in which punishment is discussed or justified in conventional discourse. The pressing problems of moderating pain and attempting to attain rational goals through punishment are never the focus of these understandings. Neither thinker aims to give a blueprint for a system of punishment, or even to justify the punishments imposed by any community, society, or state. But this only reinforces the point that all modern discussions, no matter how divergent in their conclusions, presuppose the answer to the question after which Dante and Hegel ask—the sense of pain in punishment.

One way to capture the move from Dante and Hegel into the modern age is to show a transformation in the understanding of pain that moves as follows: Whereas pain might have been understood as concomitant to the striving and desire that always defines man, a primarily spiritual experience, pain came to be seen as a bodily experience that should be eradicated from the world. Perhaps it is only natural that when the transfixing hold of the Beatitude or the Hegelian absolute is relaxed, the path to those understandings—pain—should no longer

---

51. It is interesting to note that Scarry's project focuses upon the opposite aspect of physical suffering, arguing that it is language- and world-destroying (*Body in Pain*, 13). Insofar as Scarry describes modernity's understanding of pain, she captures well a particular strand of our own thinking, but at the same time we can point to a gulf separating our own thinking from other historical understandings within our tradition.

have an honored place in human experience. If this is so, then we might add to the explanations of Spierenburg, Haskell, and Foucault that the eighteenth- and nineteenth-century humanitarian reforms were also marked by a new, even if unarticulated, understanding of pain. No longer does pain offer otherworldly promise. Further, pain is no longer a natural feature of striving prompted by a desire for the good, but comes to be seen as that which itself prompts human action. Now pain is to be measured, regulated, and, where no longer a necessity, negated. That is, the understanding of pain that comes to fruition in the modern era seems to be one generally accepted by modern writers, even when they disagree about the propriety of inflicting pain upon those being punished. Recall the competing, yet remarkably similar, accounts of pain by Newman and Christie that opened this section. But remaining to be seen are the historical developments in which this intellectual transformation in the way pain is understood play themselves out.

III

Thus far, this essay has pursued two aims: First, to frame the question concerning the relation of pain and punishment from within the contemporary sociological and historical literature in order to show its obscurity to us; second, to delineate the pronounced gulf that stands between the modern world and our heritage on this same question. This approach led to a particular characterization of a transformation in the significance of the experience of pain in punishment: Namely, that while the experience of pain in punishment once occurred in a world where that pain had a clear, intelligible, and redeeming place in the order of the world, punishment's pain came to be understood primarily as a tool imposed by an authority seeking to achieve various mundane policy goals. Pain came to be seen only as imposed from the outside, and hence both calculable and avoidable, rather than a primordial fact of the human condition.

What follows is a provisional glimpse at the penological debates that accompanied the demise of corporal punishments and ushered in the penitentiary. This glimpse is aimed only at showing, through a historical movement, how the modern understanding of pain's place in punishment came to such predominance. In advance, several features of this historical debate should be emphasized: (1) the explicit abandonment of any transcendent aims in punishment; (2) the explicit embrace of pain as a primary motivation for human action; (3) the aggregation of the conditions for redirecting human behavior into the hands of the punishing authority. While this brief catalog is by no means intended to encompass the whole of eighteenth- and nineteenth-century debates on punishment, these features do reveal how specific commitments regarding the significance of pain could come to be formulated. In the end, this account will attempt to cast, at least provisionally, new light on a well-documented historical transformation—the steady decline in the employment of painful corporal and capital punishment in the eighteenth and nineteenth centuries. Rather than appealing to a humanitarian narrative, or to Foucauldian "power/knowledge," or to some middle ground between the two, this essay suggests looking in a different direction, to a change in our understandings of pain and its place in punishment, where we can better understand the penal transformations of the modern period.

The history of the penitentiary itself, as well as the penological debates that accompany the modern prison, has been often told. Michel Foucault's account, which we looked at briefly above, is among the best-known treatments, but the literature is abundant. It is beyond our present scope to rehearse this rich history any further than a brief overview. Rather, the task of this section is to show a forgotten strand of the history of modern punishment—the place of pain in punishment.

In the late eighteenth and early nineteenth centuries prisons were transformed from largely disordered and disease-ridden buildings used primarily for the detention of debtors and accused felons awaiting trial into institutions with a specifically penal character. By the early nineteenth century, prison sentences imposed explicitly as punishments had come to replace nearly all other forms of criminal sentences. For the most part, the young American republic led the way in designing new prisons, but throughout Europe as well incarceration was embraced as the primary means of sanction. European visitors, including among others Alexis de Tocqueville from France and Charles Dickens from England, came to view the organization of American prisons and report their findings.[52]

52. Gustave de Beaumont and Alexis de Tocqueville, *On the Penitentiary System in the United States and Its Application in France,* trans. Francis Lieber (1833; New York: Augustus M. Kelley, 1970). Beaumont and Tocqueville were in many respects impressed by what they saw in American prisons, but harbored reservations concerning whether imprisonment along American models would be effective in France.

By early in the nineteenth century, the organization of American prisons came to be patterned after one of two institutional models. One was the so-called silent system. This discipline system, which as its name implied required prisoners to maintain strict silence throughout the duration of their confinement, nonetheless permitted meals and some work activity to take place in common rooms where prisoners could congregate, albeit without speaking or other communication. The other model, the so-called separate system, also required absolute silence to be observed by the prisoners, but also isolated the prisoners in individual cells where they took their meals and performed menial tasks. Very quickly, practical problems, exacerbated by the large number of convicts being sentenced to prison, made these models largely unworkable. Nonetheless, the underlying principles that recommended the silent and separate systems remained largely intact throughout the nineteenth century and even beyond. The guiding principle of the prison was the moral reformation of prisoners. The name given these institutions, after all, was quite telling—penitentiaries. The primary function of these institutions was to "conduct [the prisoner] to reformation by reflection."[53]

It should be noted that running through this language of reforming wrongdoers was a thoroughly Christian concept of repentance and moral regeneration. Religious instruction was thought by many to be an indispensable element of prison discipline. And yet there is something paradoxical here, suggesting perhaps that the religiously minded reformers were out of step with mainstream jurisprudential thought, which was, on the whole, secularized. For while prison reformers employed the language of religious regeneration, leading writers on the justification of punishment were nearly uniformly rejecting "metaphysical" or otherworldly aims for punishment. Beccaria, the standard-bearer for modern penal thought, stated plainly that the pain inflicted on a subject cannot "purge him in some metaphysical and incomprehensible way."[54] Blackstone makes clear as well the strict division that

---

On the other hand, Charles Dickens stands virtually alone among nineteenth-century observers in his dismay and even disgust at the effects of isolation and long-term confinement upon inmates. See *American Notes* (Greenwich, Conn.: Fawcett, 1843), 118–33.

53. Beaumont and Tocqueville, *On the Penitentiary System*, 3.

54. Cesare Beccaria, *Of Crimes and Punishments*, trans. Jane Grigson (New York: Marsilio, 1996), 35.

ought to be observed between metaphysical conceptions of punishment and juridical practice. "As to the end, or final cause of punishments," he writes, "[t]his is not by way of atonement or expiration for the crime committed, for that must be left to the just determination of the supreme being; but as a precaution against future offences of the same kind."[55] William Paley echoes Blackstone on this point when he says, "The proper end of human punishments is, not satisfaction of justice, but the prevention of crimes."[56]

And yet while the juristic writers were steadily bringing the aims of punishment within mundane rather than divine concerns, apologists for the penitentiary continued to speak of the spiritual reform of convicts. Sometimes, in fact, the language of reformation seemed to rest squarely in long-standing religious traditions rather than Enlightenment intellectual projects. Mary Carpenter, a noted nineteenth-century prison reformer, wrote, "In the first place, the will of the individual should be brought into such a condition as to wish to reform, and to exert itself to that end in cooperation with persons who are set over him. The state of antagonism to society must be destroyed; the hostility to divine and human law must be subdued."[57] Nearly a century earlier, Jonas Hanaway advocated that offenders be isolated in prison, where "the walls of his prison will preach peace to his soul . . . and he will confess the goodness of his maker, and the wisdom of the laws of his country."[58]

This may seem to represent an antithesis.[59] On the one hand, juristic writers such as Blackstone and Beccaria explicitly eschew any aim for punishment save the prevention of crime. Yet at the same time, prison reforms speak enthusiastically about the possibility of prison as a place for redemption and moral reformation and even salvation. Still,

---

55. William Blackstone, *Commentaries on the Laws of England* (1769; rpt. New York: Legal Classics Library, 1983), 4:11.

56. William Paley, *The Principles of Moral and Political Philosophy* (Boston: West and Richardson, 1818), 339.

57. Mary Carpenter, *Reformation Prison Discipline* (London: Longmans, Green, Reader, and Dyer, 1872), xi.

58. Cited in Randall McGowen, "The Well-Ordered Prison," in Morris and Rothman, *Oxford History of Prison*, 78.

59. The divergence between secularized Enlightenment penal reformers and those reformers who spoke from out of religious and philanthropic traditions is laid out in Adam Jay Hirsch, *The Rise of the Penitentiary: Prisons and Punishments in Early America* (New Haven: Yale University Press, 1992), 13–31.

a kinship clearly exists between those who advocated the radical secularization of punishment and those who called for spiritual regeneration. Most obviously, the kinship was grounded in a common commitment to preventing wrong. The juristic writers state this plainly:
punishment is to secure the "prevention of crimes." But this view was
clearly present in the minds of reformers as well. After all, the prisoner
whose "hostility to divine and human law" is subdued and the prisoner who comes to see "the wisdom of the laws of his country" is likely
to be the prisoner who ceases his wrongful ways.

But a deeper commitment linked the Enlightenment juristic and
religious reformers. This deeper grounding, or at least one strand of it,
was a shared understanding of the essence of the pain imposed in punishment. The language regarding pain in the paradigmatic Enlightenment era writings allows for a fairly singular articulation of the pain's
meaning. The pain of punishment had become, as Bentham put it,
"mischief" and "in itself evil."[60] Even earlier, Benjamin Franklin, in a
short treatise, had presented pain, when considered alone, as an argument against human existence: "Life," insofar as it is subject to pain, "is
not preferable to Insensibility."[61] The speculative approach to pain
taken by Franklin and Bentham is reflected also in the writings of penal
reformers. For they too evidenced a marked resistance to imposing
physical pain upon inmates. Benjamin Rush, a Quaker and leading
eighteenth-century essayist on a broad range of social practices, argued
repeatedly against the infliction of corporal punishment. While many
of his arguments were directed against the use of corporal punishment
in schools, they applied as well to penal methods. For Rush, the infliction of pain could only bring about negative results. It created in the
one punished a resentment and anger that would blunt mental faculties.[62] In agreement with Bentham, Rush casts pain solely in negative
terms, as something that created antipathy in the wrongdoer and fore-
closed the human understanding. Even where Rush was willing, albeit
reluctantly, to allow whipping as a necessary means of enforcing order

---

60. Jeremy Bentham, *The Principles of Morals and Legislation* (1781; New York:
Prometheus, 1988), 170.

61. Benjamin Franklin, *A Dissertation on Liberty and Necessity, Pain, and Pleasure*
(1733; New York: The Facsimile Text Society, 1930), 31.

62. Benjamin Rush, "An Enquiry into the Effects of Public Punishment," in *Essays:
Literary, Moral and Philosophical* (Philadelphia: Thomas and William Bradford, 1798).

(and not strictly as a punishment) in prisons, he understood the effects of the pain upon the one lashed to be only detrimental. In the following century, penal reformers echoed this feeling. The infliction of pain was, at best, a necessary evil to be used sparingly. As another advocate for the penitentiary, Dorothea Dix, would write in the nineteenth century, while she "could never order, witness, or permit its application," whipping is sometimes necessary for control of the most incorrigible prisoners, and therefore ought not be dispensed with.[63] Pain might be a necessary control mechanism applied in particular cases, but its sense was only negative, not only something any right-minded person would hate to "witness," but also something that, by its professed unintelligibility, would blunt the mind.

But even in the absence of corporal punishment, it would not be accurate to say that prison was understood as a painless environment. Indeed, as Rush noted, prison confinement was very painful. "Separation from [society]," he wrote, is "one of the severest punishments that can be inflicted upon man."[64] And recall that it was precisely this pain of separation that was meant to reform the prisoner as the walls of his cell "preached to him." It was the pain of imprisonment that provided "the facility of being moved" and that rendered prisoners "fitter for reformation."[65]

From here the kinship between the Enlightenment jurists' thinking on punishment and the stance taken by penal reformers can be seen. Pain for both was seen as an evil—necessary in extreme cases to achieve some end, but never justified in its own right. Thus, whips might be employed in prison insofar as they were necessary for order. Likewise, confinement itself was painful, but necessary to prompt the repentance and reform of criminals. In the end, the reformers seemed to confirm Bentham's opinion that "Nature has placed mankind under the governance of two sovereign masters, pain and pleasure. It is for them alone to point out what we ought to do, as well as to determine what we shall do."[66] Whereas pain had once been an emblem of the wrongdoer's will to repentance, pain now stood as a tool to prompt reformation. No longer a self-striving of the soul (as earlier thinkers had understood it),

---

63. Dorothea Dix, *Remarks on Prison and Prison Discipline in the United States* (Philadelphia: Joseph Kite, 1845), 13.

64. Rush, "Enquiry into Effects," 149.

65. Beaumont and Tocqueville, *On the Penitentiary System*, 50.

66. Bentham, *Principles of Morals*, 1.

the conditions for conformity with the law now seemed to rest solely within the hands of human authority. If the will of the offender was to be redirected toward reform, several steps, all independent of that will, needed to be taken. The most important of these steps involved isolation from society's harmful influences in solitary quietude so that repentance might begin. In a way, it seems as if these reforms attempted to appropriate the means of penitence. Through an external constraint, comprised mainly of incarcerating the individual and keeping them in complete isolation, the offender would be shown the error of his ways. By its own admission, Enlightenment ambition allowed penal reformers to facilitate and regulate the work of God. Now, brick, mortar, and time would be manipulated to cause changes in human behavior. Even the pain involved in the relationship between man and God, it seemed now, could, indeed must, be prompted and regulated by authority. But at the same time, this embracing of pain as a necessary, though deplorable, means of enforcing prison discipline seems accompanied by a radical obscurity of thought, at least in comparison to our intellectual tradition, concerning pain itself and its place in punishment.

Like the modern prison, the obscurity of our thinking regarding pain in punishment remains to this day. Indeed, as we have seen, recent scholarly accounts of the transformations in modern punishment have tended to allow the question of pain to recede from view. This obscurity becomes all the more striking when we see how distanced we are from our own traditions of thinking on the matter. The understandings of the world that once could find punishment's pain as an intelligible feature of human existence have lost the claim they once powerfully stamped upon our thinking. But pain—what it is, and the essence of our relation to it insofar as we unavoidably continue to inflict it in our punishments—remains. Perhaps, in the end, modern penal practices, from the sterility of long-term confinement to the anaesthetized methods of execution we employ, however humane they may seem to us when viewed in the historical tradition, achieve nothing more than to signal the remarkable obscurity of such questions for us.

Killing Me Softly:
Capital Punishment and the
Technologies for Taking Life

Austin Sarat

There is no law that is not inscribed on bodies. Every law has a hold
on the body. . . . Every power, including the power of law, is written
first of all on the backs of its subjects.
> —Michel de Certeau (*The Practice of Everyday Life,* 139–40)

Make a good job of this.
> —William Kemmler, first person electrocuted
> in the United States, 1891

Do they feel anything? Do they hurt? Is there any pain? Very humane
compared to what they've done to our children. The torture they've
put our kids through. I think sometimes it's too easy. They ought to
feel something. If it's fire burning all the way through their body or
whatever. There ought to be some little sense of pain to it.
> —Mother of a murder victim on being shown the planned
> method of death by lethal injection of her child's killer

People who wish to commit murder, they better not do it in the state
of Florida because we may have a problem with our electric chair.
> —Robert Butterworth, attorney general, State of
> Florida, remarking on a malfunction that
> caused a fire during an electrocution

Though our brother is on the rack . . . our sense will never inform us
of what he suffers. . . . By the imagination we place ourselves in his
situation, we conceive ourselves enduring all the same torments, we
enter as it were into his body, and become in some measure the
same person with him.
> —Adam Smith (*The Theory of the Moral Sentiments,* 9)

An earlier version of this essay appeared in Desmond Manderson, ed., *Courting Death: The Law of Mortality* (London: Pluto Press, 1999), as well as in *When the State Kills: Capital Punishment and the American Condition* (Princeton: Princeton University Press, 2001), reprinted with permission.

In March 1997 newspapers all over the United States trumpeted the "botched" electrocution of Pedro Medina, a thirty-nine-year-old Cuban immigrant convicted and condemned for the stabbing of a Florida high school teacher.[1] After the current was turned on, flames "leaped from the head" of the condemned, as one newspaper put it. "'It was horrible," a witness was quoted as saying; "'a solid flame covered his whole head, from one side to the other. I had the impression of somebody being burned alive.'"[2] Another newspaper wrote, "The electrocution of Pedro Medina on Tuesday was the stuff of nightmares and horror fiction novels and films. A foot-long blue and orange flame shot from the mask covering his head for about 10 seconds, filling the execution chamber with smoke and sickening witnesses with the odor of charred human flesh. One witness compared it to 'a burning alive.'"[3]

Yet news reports also conveyed the "reassuring" reaction of Dr. Belle Almojera, medical director at Florida State Prison, who said that before the apparatus caught fire Medina already had "lurched up in his seat and balled up his fists—the normal reaction to high voltage. . . . 'I saw no evidence of pain or suffering by the inmate throughout the entire process. In my professional opinion, he died a very quick, humane death.'"[4] The Florida Supreme Court found that "Medina's brain was instantly and massively depolarized within milliseconds of the initial surge of electricity. He suffered no conscious pain."[5] And others defended even this botched electrocution by noting that it "was much more humane than what was done to the victim."[6]

Despite these attempts to contain adverse public reaction, the Medina execution made headlines because it suggested that law's quest for a painless, and allegedly humane, technology of death was by no means complete. It did so, also, because it reminded us of the ferocity of the state's sovereign power over life itself. Yet these news stories also

---

1. See, for example, "Flames Erupt during Florida Execution: Gruesome Scene Renews Debate on Electrocutions," *USA Today*, March 26, 1997, A3.

2. "Flames Erupt in Electric Chair's Death Jolt; Execution: Fire Shoots from Florida Man's Head, Renewing Capital Punishment Debate," *Los Angeles Times*, March 26, 1997, A1.

3. "Retire 'Chair,' Use Lethal Injection," *Sun-Sentinel* (Ft. Lauderdale), March 26, 1997, A22.

4. "Inmate Catches Fire in Florida Electric Chair: 'You Could Smell the Acrid Smoke,'" *Houston Chronicle*, March 26, 1997, A6.

5. See *Jones v. Butterworth*, 701 So. 2d 76, 77 (1997).

6. "Inmate Catches Fire," A6.

contained a hint of relief for supporters of capital punishment since most treated the Medina story as a mere technological glitch rather than as an occasion to rethink the practice of state killing. Florida, the *Fort Lauderdale Sun-Sentinel* opined, "is justified in imposing the death penalty. . . . But it has no justification for retaining a method . . . that is so gruesome and violent and sometimes flawed."[7] What might have been a challenge to the legitimacy of the killing state was quickly written off to the failure of one state to keep up with the technology of the times.

Almost immediately after the Medina execution some death penalty proponents denounced electrocution as an out-of-date, unreliable technology of death and called for its replacement in Florida by lethal injection, the current technology of choice when the state kills.[8] "Under lethal injection," one newspaper explained, "the condemned is first sedated, then injected with deadly chemicals that painlessly and quickly paralyze the lungs and stop the heart."[9] As one Florida judge observed, commenting on the continuing use of electrocution in Florida, "other less cruel methods of execution are available; lethal injection is readily available . . . and is generally considered more humane."[10] In a similar vein the Florida Corrections Commission recommended a switch from electrocution to lethal injection, observing, "'Florida has an obligation to ensure that modern technologies keep pace with the level of competence in this area, and, just as changes have occurred in Florida's past in carrying out the death penalty, changes should again occur.'"[11] Several months after the Medina execution, Florida enacted legislation providing that if "electrocution is held to be unconstitutional . . . all persons sentenced to death for a capital crime shall be executed by lethal injection."[12]

---

7. "Retire Chair," A22.

8. See "Botched, Gruesome Electrocutions Mandate Switch to Lethal Injections," *Sun-Sentinel*, June 30, 1997, A8. "The voices are getting louder," the newspaper noted, "more persistent, more knowledgeable and more unified in voicing their urgent message: Florida lawmakers should abandon the electric chair for capital punishment and switch to lethal injection."

9. Ibid.

10. *Provenzano v. Moore*, Case No. 95, 973, Corrected Opinion (September 24, 1999), Supreme Court of Florida, 56.

11. Quoted in the dissenting opinion of Justice Shaw in *Provenzano*, 57.

12. Section 922.105 (1), Fla. Stat. (Supp. 1998). Electrocution will be used in Florida only on the written request of those condemned to die.

The botched execution of Pedro Medina clearly was an embarrass-
ment to a legal order seeking to put people to death, but to do it quietly,
invisibly, bureaucratically.[13] Executions, in such a system, are not supposed to make headlines. Despite statements by people like Florida's
attorney general—gruesome cruelty might, they said, be a better deterrent than death itself[14]—the Medina execution provided one of those
periodic, though increasingly rare moments, in which the state's dealing in death is thrust into the public eye. The commentary on this execution is particularly revealing in what it says about how we understand the killing state. This commentary, first, is striking for what it did
not say. Neither death itself, nor state killing, generated public horror;
there was little investment in trying to understand either what it means
for the state to deal in death, or for citizens of the United States to live
in a killing state.

That today most executions in the United States are not newswor-
thy[15] suggests that the killing state is taken for granted. If there is any
issue at all left to the public debate about capital punishment it is a
debate about *how* the state kills.[16] As the news stories about the Medina
execution suggest, the state's dealing in death is displaced by a concern
for technological efficiency in which we are invited, following Dr.
Almojera, to imagine the body as a legible text, readable for what it can
tell us about the capacity of technology to move us from life to death
swiftly, painlessly. But one might ask why the state should be concerned about the suffering of those it puts to death. Painful death might
be both more just and more effective as a deterrent than one which is
quick, quiet, and tranquil.[17]

---

13. See Robert Johnson, *Death Work: A Study of the Modern Execution Process* (Pacific
Grove, Calif.: Brooks/Cole, 1990).

14. For a fuller treatment of the connection between methods of execution and
deterrence see Jonathan Abernathy, "The Methodology of Death: Reexamining the Deterrence Rationale," *Columbia Human Rights Law Review* 27 (1996): 379.

15. There are, of course, some exceptions. Periodically controversy arises about the
appropriateness or meaning of particular executions. Thus the very public discussion of
the execution of Karla Faye Tucker, the first woman executed in the twentieth century in
Texas, focused on the question of whether her apparently deep and sincere post-convic-
tion religious conversion should be considered in deciding whether to spare her life as
well as on the question of why so few women are executed in the United States. See Rene
Heberle, "Disciplining Gender: Or, Are Women Getting Away with Murder," *Signs* 24
(1999): 1103.

16. Or sometimes about whom the state kills.

17. Abernathy argues that "contrary to what logic seems to dictate, the attempt over
time has been to make the penalty of death gentle, hidden, and antiseptic" ("The Methodology of Death," 422).

As comments by the survivors and the families of the victims in the Timothy McVeigh case suggest, there indeed is something unsettling and paradoxical in the search for a painless way of killing those who kill. McVeigh, who is scheduled to be executed on May 16, 2001, will be put to death by lethal injection. Yet the voice of vengeance demands an equivalence between pain inflicted in the crime and the pain experienced as part of the punishment. As Arlene Blanchard, a survivor of the bombing, explained after McVeigh's death sentence was handed down, "death by injection is 'too good' for McVeigh. She said he should be put in solitary confinement for life or simply hanged from a tree. 'I know it sounds uncivilized, but I want him to experience just a little of the pain and torture that he has put us through.'"[18] Or, as William Baay, an emergency worker who helped remove bodies from the Murrah building, put it, "'I don't think conventional methods should be used. They should amputate his legs with no anesthesia . . . and then set him over a bunch of bamboo shoots and let them grow up into him until he's dead.'"[19]

When law commits itself to hearing the victims' voices and to satisfying their desires for vengeance, it will be inclined toward using methods of killing that seem to many, including some of those who advocate them, "uncivilized." Thus even as it seeks to hear those voices, here too the killing state has countervailing concerns. It must find ways of distinguishing state killing from the acts to which it is a supposedly just response and to kill in such a way as not to allow the condemned to become an object of pity and, in so doing, to appropriate the status of the victim. In this essay I examine the way law seeks to balance and respond to these contradictory demands. I am concerned, in particular, about what it means for law to imagine itself to be a master of the technologies of death, or whether the relationship that is really imagined is a relationship of mastery or of subservience.

Technology mediates between the state and death. It does so in the first instance by masking physical pain and allowing the citizens to imagine that state killing is painless. But, in addition, the discursive apparatus of law works to separate cause and effect, to mask the agency responsible for execution. I argue that the search for ever more invisible, "humane" methods for state killing depends upon certain assumptions about pain and its legibility in the journey from life to

---

18. "Those Left Grief-Stricken by Bombing Cry for Vengeance," *St. Louis Post-Dispatch*, June 4, 1997, A1.

19. Ibid.

death. I am concerned, in particular, to show how the legal construction
of state killing, while it appears to reveal an assumed empathy or identification between the state and those it kills, works primarily to differentiate state killing from murder and to hierarchize the relationship
between the state and those whose lives it takes. In these efforts, we are
invited to search for a way of taking life that signals our superiority and
that marks the distinction between state violence and violence outside
the law, between a death we call capital punishment and a death we
call murder. As one commentator on the Medina execution and its
aftermath correctly observed, "Let's be honest: Seeking a 'humane'
form of execution has nothing to do with it. It is not about sparing the
condemned, but sparing ourselves. We like to keep the whole awful
business at arms length, to tell ourselves capital punishment is civilized."[20]

Doing Death Silently, Invisibly

The recent history of state killing in the United States reads like someone's idea of a story of the triumph of the idea of progress applied to
the technologies of death. From hanging to electrocution, from electrocution to lethal gas, from electricity and gas to lethal injection, the law
has moved, though not uniformly, from one technology to another.[21]
With each new invention of a technology for killing, or more precisely
with each new application of technology to killing, the law has proclaimed its own previous methods barbaric, or simply archaic. Thus, as
one judge recently said about death by electrocution, "Execution by
electrocution is a spectacle whose time has passed—like the guillotine
or public stoning or burning at the stake. . . . Florida's electric chair, by
its own track record, has proven to be a dinosaur more befitting the lab-
oratory of Baron Frankenstein than the death chamber of Florida State
Prison."[22] Responding to the advent of lethal injection, another judge
characterized the continuing use of hanging as "an ugly vestige of earlier, less civilized times when science had not yet developed medically-

---

20. "The Executioner's Weapons: After a Man Is Burned Alive in Florida's Electric
Chair, the 'New' Death Penalty Debate Focuses on the Manner in Which the Condemned
Are Put to Death," *Buffalo News*, November 9, 1997, H1, quoting columnist Leonard Pitts.
21. See Allen Huang, "Hanging, Cyanide Gas, and the Evolving Standards of
Decency: The Ninth Circuit's Misapplication of the Cruel and Unusual Clause of the
Eighth Amendment," *Oregon Law Review* 74 (1995): 995.
22. Dissenting opinion by Justice Shaw in *Jones*, 87.

appropriate methods of bringing human life to an end."[23] Nothing but the best will do in the business of state killing.[24]

This search for a technological fix contrasts markedly with the execution business of another era. Historically executions were, in Foucault's words, "More than an act of justice"; they were a "manifestation of force."[25] They were always centrally about display, in particular the display of the majestic, awesome power of sovereignty as it was materialized on the body of the condemned. Public executions functioned as public theater, but also as a school for citizenship.[26] Choosing the right method to kill was a matter of sovereign prerogative. Methods were chosen for their ability to convey the ferocity of the sovereign's vengeance.

The act of execution helped constitute citizens as subjects. On Foucault's account state killing produced a sadistic relation between the executioner, the victim, and the audience. The pleasure of viewing, as well as the instruction in one's relation to sovereign power, was to be found in witnessing pain inflicted. The excesses of execution and the enthusiastic response of the attending crowd blended the performance of torture with pleasure, creating an unembarrassed celebration of death that knew no law except the law of one person's will materialized on the body of the condemned. The display of violence, of the sovereignty that was constituted in killing, was designed to create fearful, if not obedient, subjects.[27]

The act of putting someone to death contained a dramatic, awe-inspiring pedagogy of power. "The public execution," Foucault explained,

> has a juridico-political function. It is a ceremonial by which a momentarily injured sovereignty is reconstituted. It restores sovereignty by manifesting it at its most spectacular. The public execution, however hasty and everyday, belongs to a whole series of

---

23. Judge Reinhardt dissenting in *Campbell v. Wood*, 18 F.3d 662, 701 (1994).

24. For one example of this phenomenon see Thomas Metzger, *Blood and Volts: Edison, Tesla, and the Electric Chair* (Brooklyn: Autonomedia, 1996).

25. Michel Foucault, *Discipline and Punish*, trans. Alan Sheridan (New York: Vintage, 1977), 50.

26. See Pieter Spierenburg, *The Spectacle of Suffering* (Cambridge: Cambridge University Press, 1984).

27. See V. A. C. Gatrell, *The Hanging Tree: Execution and the English People, 1770–1868* (New York: Oxford University Press, 1994), chap. 2.

great rituals in which power is eclipsed and restored (coronation, entry of the king into a conquered city, the submission of rebellious subjects). . . . There must be an emphatic affirmation of power and its intrinsic superiority. And this superiority is not simply that of right, but that of the physical strength of the sovereign beating down upon the body of his adversary and mastering it.[28]

Doing death was precisely about the right of the state to kill as it pleased. Sovereignty was known, as Locke reminds us, in and through acts of taking life.[29] Executions were designed to make the state's dealing in death majestically visible to all.[30] Live, but live by the grace of the sovereign; live but remember that your life belongs to the state: these were the messages of the state killing of an earlier era.

Without a public audience state killing would have been meaningless. As Foucault put it, "Not only must the people know, they must see with their own eyes. Because they must be made afraid, but also because they must be witnesses, the guarantors of the punishment, and because they must to a certain extent take part in it."[31] In this understanding of the relationship of punishment and the people, "the role of the people was an ambiguous one."[32] They were, at one and the same time, fearful subjects, authorizing witnesses, and lustful participants.

Today the death penalty, with some notable exceptions, has been transformed from dramatic spectacle to cool, bureaucratic operation, and the role of the public now is strictly limited and strictly controlled.[33] The modern execution is carried out behind prison walls in what amounts to semiprivate, sacrificial ceremonies in which a few selected witnesses are gathered in a carefully controlled situation to see, and in their seeing to sanctify, the state's taking of the life of one of its citizens. As Richard Johnson suggests,

> In the modern period (from 1800 on), ceremony gradually gave way to bureaucratic procedure played out behind prison walls, in

---

28. Foucault, *Discipline and Punish*, 48–49.

29. John Locke, *Second Treatise of Government*, ed. Thomas Peardon (Indianapolis: Bobbs-Merrill, 1952), 4.

30. Gatrell, *The Hanging Tree*.

31. Foucault, *Discipline and Punish*, 58.

32. Ibid.

33. See Johnson, *Death Work*.

isolation from the community. Feelings are absent, or at least suppressed, in bureaucratically administered executions. With bureaucratic procedure, there is a functional routine dominated by hierarchy and task. Officials perform mechanistically before a small, silent gathering of authorized witnesses.[34]

Capital punishment becomes, at best, a hidden reality. It is known, if it is known at all, by indirection.[35] As Hugo Bedau puts it, "The relative privacy of executions nowadays (even photographs of the condemned man dying are almost invariably strictly prohibited) means that the average American literally does not know what is being done when the government, in his name and presumably on his behalf, executes a criminal."[36] What was public is now private. What was high drama has been reduced to a matter of technique.

Whereas once the technologies of killing deployed by the state were valued precisely because of their gruesome effects on the body of the condemned, today we seek a technology that leaves no trace.[37] Whereas in the past the technologies were valued as ways of making the sovereign power awe-inspiring and fearsome, today the process of state killing is medicalized; it is less about sovereignty than science. As Madow notes,

Executions were progressively stripped of their ritualistic and religious aspects. . . . [A]s Americans developed a keen dread of physical pain, medical professionals teamed up with . . . engineers to devise a purportedly "painless" method of administering the death penalty. . . . The condemned man . . . had now become simply the object of medico-bureaucratic technique—his body read closely for signs of pain. . . . The overriding aim of the state functionaries charged with conducting executions nowadays is to "get

34. Ibid., 5. Also Susan Blaustein, "Witness to Another Execution," *Harper's*, May 1994, 53; and Richard Trombley, *The Execution Protocol: Inside America's Capital Punishment Industry* (New York: Crown, 1992).

35. See Foucault, *Discipline and Punish*, chap. 1. Also Jacques Derrida, "Force of Law: The 'Mystical Foundation of Authority,'" *Cardozo Law Review* 11 (1990): 925.

36. See Hugo Adam Bedau, *The Death Penalty in America* (New York: Oxford University Press, 1982), 13.

37. Blaustein, "Witness to Another Execution."

the man dead" as quickly, uneventfully, impersonally, and painlessly as Nature and Science permit.[38]   .

Since the earliest recorded execution in the America in 1608, more
than sixteen thousand people have been put to death at the hands of the
state.[39] "We've sawed people in half, beheaded them, burned them,
drowned them, crushed them with rocks, tied them to anthills, buried
them alive, and [executed them] in almost every way except perhaps
boiling them in oil."[40] Today, however, five methods of execution are
currently available, firing squad, hanging, lethal gas, electrocution, and
lethal injection. The first two are authorized in just a few states, six
states use lethal gas, four more authorize electrocution as the sole
method of state killing, and lethal injection is available in thirty-four
states.[41]

When, in 1888, New York became the first state to institute death
by electrocution, it did so because an expert commission found it to be
"the most humane and practical method known to modern science of
carrying into effect the sentence of death."[42] States that eventually followed New York's lead "viewed . . . [electrocution] as less painful than
hanging and less horrific than having the condemned swing from the
gallows."[43] States that rejected hanging in favor of the gas chamber
viewed it as "more decent" than electrocution since it seemed less violent and did not mutilate the body.[44] Thus the original legislation
authorizing the use of gas stipulated that the condemned was to be put
to death, "without warning and while asleep in his cell."[45]

These same concerns have been echoed in the most recent fad
among the technologies of state killing, lethal injection.[46] Upholding

---

38. Michael Madow, "Forbidden Spectacle: Executions, the Public, and the Press in
Nineteenth-Century New York," *Buffalo Law Review* 43 (1995): 466, 469.

39. Huang, "Hanging, Cyanide Gas," 997.

40. Ian Gray and Moira Stanley, *A Punishment in Search of a Crime: Americans Speak
Out Against The Death Sentence* (New York: Avon Books, 1989), 19–20.

41. The numbers add up to more than thirty-eight (the number of states using capital punishment) because statutes often permit more than one means of execution.

42. Quoted in *In re Kemmler*, 136 U.S. 436, 444 (1890).

43. Abernathy, "The Methodology of Death," 404.

44. Ibid.

45. William Bowers with Glenn L. Pierce and John F. McDevitt, *Legal Homicide:
Death as Punishment in America, 1864–1982* (Boston : Northeastern University Press, 1984),
12.

46. Raymond Paternoster, *Capital Punishment in America* (New York: Lexington,
1991), 23.

the constitutionality of lethal injection, a federal district court recently noted, "There is general agreement that lethal injection is at present the most humane type of execution available and is far preferable to the sometimes barbaric means employed in the past."[47] This is hardly the language of either the survivors and families of the victims of the Oklahoma City bombing or the awe-inspiring sovereignty about which Foucault wrote. Still one might ask what is at stake in state killing when the state imagines itself killing decently, painlessly, humanely.

On the Invisible Body of the Condemned

Cases challenging the constitutionality of particular methods of execution are regularly, though not frequently, brought before courts in the United States.[48] In the first two such cases to reach the United States Supreme Court, the Court upheld first the use of firing squads[49] and then electrocution as a means through which the state could take life.[50] In the latter case, the Court proclaimed that no method of execution could be used that would "involve torture or a lingering death."[51] The Court went on to say that the state could kill so long as it used methods that did not impose "something more than the mere extinguishment of life."[52]

This is quite a remarkable sentence, remarkable in the casual way in which it purports to limit sovereign prerogative, in the juxtaposition of the word "mere" with an awkward circumlocution for death, and in its seeming acquiescence in the view that "mere" death at the hands of the state gives no grounds for complaint. It condemns excess, "something more," as if state-imposed death itself was not already an excess

---

47. See *Hill vs. Lockhart*, 791 F. Supp. 1388, 1394 (1992). See also *Ex Parte Kenneth Granviel*, 561 S.W. 2d 503, 513 (1978). The court found that the "Texas Legislature substituted death by lethal injection as a means of execution in lieu of electrocution for the reason it would be a more humane and less spectacular form of execution." As Justice Anstead argued in *Provenzano*, "[J]ust as electrocution may have been originally evaluated in comparison with hanging, we know today that the overwhelming majority of death penalty jurisdictions have long since rejected use of the electric chair and have turned to lethal injection as a more humane punishment" (70–71).

48. Kristina Beard, "Five under the Eighth: Methodology Review and the Cruel and Unusual Punishments Clause," *University of Miami Law Review* 51 (1997): 445.

49. *Wilkinson v. Utah*, 99 U.S. 130 (1878).

50. *In re Kemmler.*

51. Ibid., 447.

52. Ibid.

that marks the limits of the state's sovereignty over life.[53] The state can spare life, or extinguish it, but it cannot require its victims to "linger" between life and death. Law stands ready to police the excesses of sovereignty, but it still grants sovereignty its due. The domain of sovereignty extends to deciding who shall die and to death-imposing acts; what is left for law is to police the technologies through which the state takes life.

Sometimes, however, even this jurisdiction has seemed more than the law could, or would, handle. Indeed, more often than not, the law has stayed its hand in the face of allegations about the excesses of the state's dealing in death. Perhaps the most famous instance of such inaction occurred in *Francis v. Resweber*,[54] a case in which the United States Supreme Court allowed the state of Louisiana to execute a convicted murderer twice.[55] As the Court recounted the relevant facts, "Francis was prepared for execution and on May 3, 1946 . . . was placed in the official electric chair of the State of Louisiana . . . The executioner threw the switch but, presumably because of some mechanical difficulty, death did not result."[56] Sometime later Francis sought to prevent a "second" execution by contending that it would constitute cruel and unusual punishment.[57]

Justice Reed, writing for a majority of the Court, responded to these claims in what initially appears to be a rather unusual way. For him the cruelty of Louisiana's plan had little to do with Francis,[58] any

---

53. See Giorgio Agamben, *Homo Sacer: Sovereign Power and Bare Life*, trans. Daniel Heller-Roazen (Stanford: Stanford University Press, 1998), 83. As Peter Fitzpatrick puts it, "Law maintains its appeal to an-other by always being more than determined, by being ever able to be otherwise than what it determinedly is. One day to come . . . , law could actually be more and extend to the previously excluded. Death denies that promise. . . . So, in dealing death, law makes irremediable the exclusions that have gone to make it what it is." "'Always More to Do': Capital Punishment and the (De)Composition of Law," in *The Killing State: Capital Punishment in Law, Politics, and Culture*, ed. Austin Sarat (New York; Oxford University Press, 1999), 128–29.

54. *Francis v. Resweber*, 329 U.S. 459 (1947).

55. For an interesting description of the case see Arthur Miller and Jeffrey Bowman, *Death by Installments: The Ordeal of Willie Francis* (Westport, Conn.: Greenwood Press, 1988).

56. See *Francis*, 460 n. 12.

57. Francis also alleged that a second execution would violate the due process clause of the Fourteenth Amendment (ibid., 462).

58. Indeed Willie Francis makes virtually no appearance in Reed's opinion. We learn little about him except that he was a "colored citizen of Louisiana" (ibid., at 460). Neglect of the real life experiences and feelings of the people whose fate is decided by law is characteristic of a wide range of legal decisions. See John Noonan, *Persons and Masks of the Law* (New York: Farrar, Straus and Giroux, 1976).

pain he might have suffered during the first execution and his painful anticipations of the second. The Constitution, as Reed understood it, clearly permits "the *necessary* suffering involved in any method employed to extinguish life humanely" (emphasis added).[59] Note how in Reed's formulation some suffering, suffering deemed "necessary," is fully compatible with humane killing. Something more than the mere extinction of life is permissible so long as that excess inheres in the "method" and so long as it is impossible for the state to kill without it.

What the Constitution permits, dutiful judges, on Reed's account, should not prohibit. If Francis had to undergo a second, more lethal, dose of electricity, it was because the rules, not the judges, allow it. According to those rules, the fact of the first, unsuccessful execution would not "add an element of cruelty to a subsequent execution."[60] The constitutional question, as Reed saw it, turned instead on the behavior of those in charge of Francis's "first" execution, those authorized to unleash state violence. Their acts and intentions were decisive in determining whether a second execution would be unconstitutionally cruel.

From the facts as he understood them, Reed found those officials to have carried out their duties in a "careful and humane manner" with "no suggestion of malevolence"[61] and no "purpose to inflict unnecessary pain."[62] He described diligent, indeed even compassionate, executioners frustrated by what he labeled an "unforeseeable accident . . . for which no man is to blame," and concluded that the state itself would be unfairly punished were it deprived of a second chance to execute Francis.[63] Indeed in the only place where Reed tries to come to terms with what the first execution did to Francis he suggests, again relying on the image of the first execution as an accident, that Francis could only have suffered "the identical amount of mental anguish and physical pain [as

---

59. *Francis,* 464.

60. Ibid.

61. Ibid., 462.

62. Ibid.

63. Ibid., 464. It is clear (or clear enough) where Reed wanted to come out: unforeseeable accidents cannot be regarded as "inherent" in any method of punishment (including electrocution); on the other hand, every method (including electrocution) is susceptible to such accidents. But this distinction, clear though it may be, sheds no light at all on why "unforeseeable accidents" that cause extraneous pain do not constitute the kind of cruel and unusual punishment that the Eighth Amendment forbids. As Justice Burton's dissent points out, "the intent of the executioner cannot lessen the torture or excuse the result" (ibid., 477). Moreover, Reed provides no reason for thinking that the state must be found blameworthy before its punishments can be declared cruel and unusual.

in] any other occurrence, such as . . . a fire in the cell block."[64] While Reed described Francis as an "accident victim," the issue for Francis was the future as much as the past. For him what was constitutionally significant was the connection between the violence inflicted on him during the first execution and the violence the state, with the Supreme Court's blessing, proposed to inflict on him in a second execution.

So remote was the Court's interest in Francis, in the death it was condoning, or in the pain that he had already experienced and would again experience, that only late in the dissenting opinion of Justice Burton was any reference made to the effect of the first execution attempt on Francis himself.[65] There we are told that his "lips puffed out and he groaned and jumped so that the chair came off the floor."[66] Nonetheless, even here the significance of Francis's impending death is deferred, as is his pain. References to that pain, taken from affidavits by witnesses to the first execution, were included solely to point out a "conflict in testimony"[67] that made it impossible, in Burton's view, to determine whether any electricity actually had reached Francis during the abortive execution attempt. The conflict to which Burton refers involves whether any electric current actually reached Francis's body during the first execution attempt and arose when those in charge of the electrical equipment testified that "no electrical current reached . . . (Francis) and that his flesh did not show electrical burns."[68]

Burton did worry about the number of failed executions the majority might tolerate before declaring subsequent attempts to be cruel and unusual. Yet while he labeled the state's desire to carry out a second execution "death by installments,"[69] most of his opinion was devoted to a careful scrutiny of Louisiana's death penalty statute. Death itself is not the object of attention. Instead Burton seeks to affirm the possibility of law's mastery over death as well as law's fidelity to its own rules for taking life. A proper execution is one whose occasions and procedures are prescribed by law, just as a proper judgment is one governed by the law and the law alone. Since the statute made no provision for "a sec-

---

64. Ibid., 464.
65. It is perhaps noteworthy that this reference is relegated to a footnote.
66. Ibid., 480 n. 2.
67. Ibid., 480.
68. See ibid., 481 n. 2.
69. Ibid., 474.

ond, third or multiple application of (electric) current,"[70] a second execution should not, in Burton's opinion, be permitted. Though differing as to the correct result, Burton joined Reed in severing the connection between their acts of judgment and the fate of Willie Francis. They both treated the behavior of the state rather than the experience, and prospective death, of its intended victim as constitutionally significant.

The way both Burton and Reed proceeded in *Francis* seems, in the end, all too familiar and yet, from the perspective of the reactions to the Medina execution, somewhat strange. In *Francis*, death, the very business of the case, is but a shadowy presence, barely acknowledged. Where it is inadvertently glimpsed, Francis's return date with electrocution is presented as the deed of some abstract, impersonal set of written rules; the judge's own hand is stayed. In the opinions of both Burton and Reed, death is the absent subject, but so is pain and the search for a humane way of killing.

The "Body in Pain"

Today death still appears to be the absent subject when courts confront challenges to the state's technologies of death. However, unlike in the *Francis* case, where the question of pain was almost completely elided, courts faced with challenges to the state's technologies for taking life now focus, almost obsessively, on that question.[71] They sometimes treat the body as a legible text on which can be read the signs of excess, the signs that the state's chosen method imposes something more than the mere extinction of life. At other times, however, they seek to read pain indirectly, hardly mentioning the body at all. Yet the law's increasing obsession with pain is really an obsession with pain as it appears to those who serve as witnesses, real or imagined, of state killing. It is the experience of execution by its witnesses, and a concern for their "suffering," that fuels the search for painless death.

Let me focus on three recent examples to highlight this continuity and this difference. The first, *Campbell v. Wood*,[72] decided in 1994, dealt with the constitutionality of hanging as a method of execution; the sec-

---

70. Ibid., 475.

71. See Alan Hyde, *Bodies of Law* (Princeton, N.J.: Princeton University Press, 1997), chap. 11.

72. *Campbell v. Wood*, 18 F.3d 662 (1994).

ond, *Fierro v. Gomez*,[73] decided later that same year, dealt with execution by lethal gas; the third, a 1999 decision of the Florida State Supreme Court, *Provenzano v. Moore*,[74] concerned the constitutionality of electrocution. The former upheld the use of hanging; the second prohibited the state of California from using gas to kill; the third found that death in the electric chair did not violate the Constitution.

Judge Beezer, writing for the majority in *Campbell*, framed the question presented in that case as "whether hanging comports with contemporary standards of decency."[75] He noted that, while few states now use hanging, no court in the United States had ever found execution by hanging to violate the Constitution. Nor, in his view, does the "mere" fact that hanging causes death render it unconstitutional. Instead Beezer argued that the question of whether hanging was acceptable depended on "the actual pain that may or may not attend the practice."[76] Determining the constitutionality of this method of execution required the court to engage in a complex semiotic activity, to read the body of the condemned for what it reveals of its suffering as it moves from the world of the living to the world of the dead. Beezer took note of the fact that the district court had heard extensive expert and eyewitness testimony concerning the way hanging causes death and the pain that is associated with it.[77] He wrote confidently about the court's ability to know the pain of the condemned even as he noted that pain itself would not render hanging invalid. A method of execution, he claimed, relying on *Kemmler* and *Francis*, is only unconstitutional if it "involves the unnecessary and wanton infliction of pain."[78]

With this as the standard, Beezer provided an extended discussion of the methods used in hanging, contrasting in particular the "long-drop" with the "short-drop" method.[79] He found that several factors contribute to making death by hanging "comparatively painless,"[80] for

---

73. *Fierro v. Gomez*, 865 F. Supp. 1387 (1994).

74. Case No. 95, 973, Corrected Opinion (September 24, 1999), Supreme Court of Florida.

75. *Campbell*, 682.

76. Ibid.

77. For a discussion of that hearing claiming that "the question of whether hanging is a form of cruel and unusual punishment is curiously absent," see Timothy Kaufman-Osborne, "'The Metaphysics of the Hangman,'" *Studies in Law, Politics, and Society* 20 (2000): 35.

78. Ibid., 683.

79. Ibid.

80. Ibid., 684.

example, the length of the drop, the selection and treatment of the rope, the positioning of the knot. Washington's use of the long-drop method of hanging, he said, is designed "to ensure that forces to the neck structures are optimized to cause rapid unconsciousness and death."[81] The result of the methods deployed in Washington, Beezer argued, was that "unconsciousness and death . . . occur extremely rapidly, that unconsciousness was likely to be immediate or within a matter of seconds, and that death would follow rapidly thereafter."[82] He ended his opinion by reiterating that "Campbell is not entitled to a painless execution, but only one free of purposeful cruelty."[83]

Here Beezer seems to return us, at least partially, to the world of *Francis*, in which attention moves from the executed to the executioner, from the body in pain to the intentions of the executioner.[84] But there is a crucial difference; unlike in *Francis*, where the subject of pain is almost completely avoided, in *Campbell* determining the pain associated with one or another technology of death is always a necessary, though not sufficient, first step. If such a determination suggests that the condemned is subject to pain, the court must then, but only then, inquire into the purposes of the state in imposing death through that method. Evidence of pain suggests barbarism on the part of those who take life. Pain is thus the dangerous supplement of death, signaling as it does excess or the sadistic pleasure associated with the willful taking of human life.

Judge Reinhardt dissented from Beezer's view in *Campbell* because it seemed to equate the "evolving standard of decency" of Eighth Amendment jurisprudence solely with an inquiry into pain and its purposes. In his view the development of "new and less brutal methods of execution, such as lethal injection" as well as the "risks of pain and mutilation inherent in hanging" make it constitutionally defective.[85] The fact that, by the time of *Campbell*, all but a few state legislatures had abolished hanging provided, for Reinhardt, an additional but still crucial indicator of its incompatibility with contemporary standards of decency. Moreover, if the reduction of needless pain were to be taken as the exclusive measure of a technique's constitutionality, "barbaric

---

81. Ibid.
82. Ibid., 687.
83. Ibid.
84. See Huang, "Hanging, Cyanide Gas."
85. *Campbell*, 693.

and savage" forms of punishment such as the guillotine would not be constitutionally impermissible.

In the end, even if the Constitution were to mandate only an objective inquiry into pain and its purposes, judicial hanging would still, in Reinhardt's view, be unacceptable because it is "a crude, rough, and wanton procedure, the purpose of which is to tear apart the spine. It is needlessly violent and intrusive, deliberately degrading and dehumanizing. It causes grievous fear beyond that of death itself and the attendant consequences are often humiliating and disgusting."[86] It carries with it a "high risk of pain far more than is necessary to kill a condemned inmate. If the drop is too short, the prisoner will strangle to death, a slow and painful process. . . . [If the drop] is too long the prisoner may be decapitated."[87]

A punishment can be cruel, Reinhardt contended, even if it is not painful. Cruelty can arise "from the relatively painless infliction of degradation, savagery, and brutality. . . . Indignities can be inflicted even after a person has died."[88] The Constitution *obligates* the state, when it chooses to kill, to "eliminate the degrading, brutal, and violent aspects of an execution, and substitute a scientifically developed and approved method of terminating life through appropriate medical procedures in a neutral, medical environment."[89] Where science makes available technologies for ending life that serve the same goals, but with markedly lower risk of imposing pain, the Constitution *requires* that the state follow science. On Reinhardt's reading, the state is not master of technology; it is instead subservient to it. Whereas Beezer imposed few limits on the sovereign's choice of the method of execution, Reinhardt would eliminate much, if not all, of the sovereign's discretion.

While Beezer and Reinhardt differ on the sufficiency of pain as a standard in determining the constitutionality of a method of execution, both assume that they can know the pain of another and that they can represent it faithfully in their opinions. As Reinhardt put it, "There is absolutely no question that every hanging involves a risk that the prisoner will not die immediately, but will instead struggle or asphyxiate to death. This process, which may take several minutes, is extremely

---

86. Ibid., 701.
87. Ibid., 708.
88. Ibid., 702.
89. Ibid.

painful. Not only does the prisoner experience the pain felt by any strangulation victim, but he does so while dangling at the end of a rope."[90] Though neither Beezer nor Reinhardt may know, or be able to accurately represent, death, they write with no hesitancy about their ability to know the pain that precedes it.

This apparent displacement of death as well as this same confidence in the court's ability to read and represent pain is seen in *Fierro*. Judge Patel notes, early in her *Fierro* opinion, that while lethal gas had been the execution technology of choice in California since 1937, in the mid-1980s Warden Vasquez of San Quentin revised the state's execution protocol. This statement takes on significance later in her decision when it is linked to the kind of technological imperative hinted at in Reinhardt's opinion in *Campbell*. As Patel put it, neither the warden nor his staff "consulted scientific experts or medical personnel in formulating the execution protocol nor did they examine records from previous California executions."[91] The result is characterized as an "unscientific, slapdash" execution protocol.[92] When sovereignty exercises its power over life and death, it is not free to kill in a gruesome way in order to instill awe and fear in the citizenry. The availability of lethal injection, which Patel characterized as "more humane than lethal gas as a method of execution," renders the latter "antiquated" and incompatible with the Constitution.[93] Rather than being the master of technology, law requires that sovereignty be its servant.

Taking *Campbell* as governing authority in the *Fierro* case, Patel characterized it as making "clear" that the "key question to be answered in a challenge to the method of execution is how much pain the inmate suffers."[94] *Campbell*, she argued, "dictates that a court look first to objective evidence of pain."[95] After providing an elaborate description of the gas chamber and the procedures used during an execution by lethal gas, Patel reviewed contradictory expert testimony concerning the effects of lethal gas and the precise ways it brings about death.

As she summarized it, the basic disagreement between plaintiff

---

90. Ibid., 712.
91. *Fierro*, 1391.
92. Ibid., 1413.
93. Ibid., 1407.
94. Ibid., 1410–11.
95. Ibid., 1412.

and defense experts is "whether unconsciousness occurs within at most thirty seconds of inhalation, as defendants maintain, or whether, as plaintiffs contend, unconsciousness occurs much later, after the inmate has endured the painful effects of cyanide gas for several minutes."[96] To resolve this conflict, she reviewed extant scientific literature but determined that, while "plaintiffs' theory of death through cellular suffocation has traditionally been the accepted viewpoint,"[97] the scientific community was neither uniform nor clear in its conclusions.

Next Patel reviewed two types of eyewitness accounts of execution by lethal injection. The first, the contemporaneous observations and records of physicians who attended every execution by lethal gas, reads like an obsessive archive of death. It provides space for the physician to record when, during the course of an execution, each of the following events occur: " 'Sodium Cyanide Enters'; 'Gas Strikes Prisoner's Face'; 'Prisoner Apparently Unconscious'; and 'Prisoner Certainly Unconscious' and 'Last Bodily Movement.' "[98] The other type of eyewitness evidence were observations by lay witnesses.

Patel prefaced her discussion of all of this evidence by noting that "neither consciousness nor pain is easy to gauge. Actions that appear volitional or appear to be a reaction to pain may in fact be unconscious and non-volitional."[99] Yet these cautions did not inhibit her interpretation of the observational testimony. Pain, while difficult to measure, could in her view, be read on the surface of the body, by untrained people as well as by medical personnel. Their observations provide the measure for constitutional judgment.

Beginning with California's two most recent executions, Patel noted that the physicians' records revealed that "certain unconsciousness" did not occur until three minutes after the gas hit the face of the condemned. Records of California's earlier executions contain similar results. Taken together, the expert testimony, the scientific literature, the physicians' records and eyewitness statements "compel" and "unmistakably"[100] point, according to the judge, to the conclusion that during a period of consciousness following the dispensing of lethal gas that "inmates suffer intense, visceral pain, primarily as a result of lack

96. Ibid., 1396.
97. Ibid., 1398.
98. Ibid., 1401.
99. Ibid., 1400.
100. Ibid., 1403.

of oxygen to the cells."[101] This pain, Patel asserted, moving from calm balancing of evidence to vivid analogy, is "akin to the experience of a major heart attack, or to being held under water."[102] In this resort to analogy Patel sought to conjure imagined horrors somewhat closer to home for the average citizen than the particular horrors associated with death in the gas chamber.

Like both Judges Beezer and Reinhardt in *Campbell*, Patel foregrounds the question of what the journey from life to death might be under one particular execution technique. She too focuses on the presence of pain, carefully constructing a narrative from different strands of evidence. She insists that the state kill as softly, as gently, as painlessly as the minds of men and women allow.[103]

Her opinion, like the opinions in *Campbell*, textualizes pain, sometimes by focusing on the body of the condemned and sometimes by reading through it to understand consciousness and its limits. A similar strategy was followed by the majority in *Provenzano*,[104] which began by examining alleged errors in previous executions, in particular the execution of Allen Lee Davis. "Allen Lee Davis," the court claimed, "did not suffer any conscious pain while being electrocuted in Florida's electric chair. Rather he suffered instantaneous and painless death once the current was applied to him."[105] The *Provenzano* majority cautioned against misreading the body, saying "The nose bleed incurred by Allen Lee Davis began *before* the electric current was applied to him, and was not caused whatsoever by the application of electrical current to Davis."[106] It noted that "the record in this case reveals abundant evidence that execution by electrocution renders an inmate instantaneously unconscious, thereby making it impossible to feel pain."[107] Because it is painless, the court concluded, death by electrocution is not cruel and because it is not cruel it is not unconstitutional.

Justice Shaw, in his dissent, agreed, at least in part, about the cen-

---

101. Ibid., 1404.

102. Ibid.

103. This approach was recently followed in another case that found lethal gas to be unconstitutional in Arizona. See *LaGrand v. Stewart*, 173 F.3d 1144 (1999).

104. This case is only one of a several recent cases in which Florida courts were confronted with challenges to electrocution. See, for example, *Jones* and *Buenoano v. State*, 565 So. 2d 309 (1990).

105. *Provenzano*, 3.

106. Ibid.

107. Ibid., 4.

trality of pain, though he reached strikingly different conclusions about its presence when electrocution is the method of state killing, reminding us that legibility of the pain does not ensure that its presence will be recognized by all its readers. But, like Reinhardt in *Campbell*, he insisted that the courts should not focus obsessively and exclusively on pain as the sole indicator of cruelty. Of particular importance here was the question of what he labeled "violence, mutilation, and disgrace."[108]

Choosing the guillotine as his example, he expressed a breezy confidence in his ability to read pain when he noted, "while beheading results in a quick, relatively painless death, it entails frank violence (i.e. gross laceration and blood-letting) and mutilation (i.e. decapitation), and disgrace . . . and thus is facially cruel."[109] Pain as well as violence, mutilation, and disgrace, Shaw claimed, accompany electrocution. "Not only was every execution in Florida accompanied by the inevitable convulsing and burning that characterizes electrocution, but further, three executions were marred by extraordinary violence and mutilation. In two . . . , smoke and flames spurted from the headpiece and burned the heads and faces of the inmates. In the third execution, the inmate bled from the nostrils and was at least partially asphyxiated by the restraining devices; and he too was burned."[110]

Shaw's opinion goes on for pages providing elaborate, detailed, and graphic descriptions of those three executions, paying particular attention to the third, the Davis execution. But, in an extraordinary gesture, he appended to his opinion "post-execution color photos of Davis before he was removed from the electric chair. These photos . . . provide a vivid picture of a violent scene . . . [and] show a ghastly post-execution scene."[111] (See photographs following page 90.) While he provided his own verbal description of what those photographs show ("a stream of blood pours from his nostrils, flows over the wide-leather mouthstrap, runs down his neck and chest, and forms a bright red pool . . . on his white shirt"),[112] the photographic evidence was meant to speak for itself. Appending such images to a judicial opinion transgresses convention in such a way as to ensure that they will be the subject of considerable attention and commentary. They shock and appeal to a dif-

---

108. Ibid., 34.
109. Ibid., 38.
110. Ibid., 43.
111. Ibid., 47 and 51.
112. Ibid., 52.

ferent register of understanding. They make pain and the violence associated with state killing into a matter of sight. Because they are "vivid," Shaw assumed that they would convey a reality made more transparent than any language could convey. Thus the presence of the photos is not only an almost unprecedented judicial effort to make state killing visible, it is also a stark reminder of the limits of language when it speaks about physical violence and physical pain.[113]

Pain, as Elaine Scarry argues,

> has no voice. . . . When one hears about another's physical pain, the events happening within the interior of that person's body may seem to have the remote character of some deep subterranean fact, belonging to an invisible geography that, however portentous, has no reality because it has not yet manifested itself on the visible surface of the earth.[114]

Pain is, according to Scarry,

> [v]aguely alarming yet unreal, laden with consequence yet evaporating before the mind because not available to sensory confirmation. . . . [U]nseeable classes of objects such as subterranean plates, Seyfert galaxies, and the pains occurring in other people's bodies flicker before the mind, then disappear. . . . [Pain] achieves . . . its aversiveness in part by bringing about, even within the radius of several feet, this absolute split between one's sense of one's own reality and the reality of other persons. . . . Whatever pain achieves, it achieves in part through its unsharability, and it ensures this unsharability through its resistance to language.[115]

"A great deal is at stake," Scarry herself suggests, "in the attempt to invent linguistic structures that will reach and accommodate this area of experience normally so inaccessible to language."[116] The cases on methods of execution surely confirm this view. Yet Scarry reminds

---

113. Turning to the visual does not resolve these problems. Indeed the seeming "transparency" of photographs of death creates its own difficulties.

114. Elaine Scarry, *The Body in Pain: The Making and Unmaking of the World* (New York: Oxford University Press), 3.

115. Ibid., 4.

116. Ibid., 6.

us that the capacity of courts to understand and to convey the pain of
the person being executed to their readers is quite limited, even as this
capacity is foregrounded in these cases.

Scarry invites us to consider legal cases like *Francis, Campbell,
Fierro,* and *Provenzano* as occasions for lawyers and judges to "invent"
languages of violence and pain. However, she suggests that in law, as
elsewhere, the languages that can be invented are quite limited. "As
physical pain is monolithically consistent in its assault on language,"
Scarry writes, "so the verbal strategies for overcoming the assault are
very small in number and reappear consistently as one looks at the
words of the patient, physician, Amnesty worker, lawyer, artist."[117]
Those verbal strategies "revolve around the verbal sign of the
weapon."[118] We know pain, in the first instance, through its instrumen-
talities, for example, hanging or lethal gas. Second, we know it through
its effects. Here violence and pain are represented in the "wound," that
is, "the bodily damage that is pictured as accompanying pain."[119] But,
as Scarry suggests, these representations can provide no certain or reliable grounding for a jurisprudence that seeks to govern the technologies through which the state puts people to death. Yet it is precisely
those representations that play a central role in death penalty jurisprudence.

If Scarry is right, then the courts in the United States have created
for themselves epistemological and interpretive as well as legal and
political problems. By deferring the question of death and foreground-
ing the question of pain they are required to take seriously the empirical world of the body and its suffering even as they necessarily run up
against the limits of their capacity to know that world and to render it
in language.[120] Yet again we are driven back to the question of why the
question of pain and the search for painless execution play so large a
part in the law's confrontation with the killing state.

---

117. Ibid., 13.
118. Ibid., 15.
119. Ibid.

120. The movement from representing death to representing pain as the touchstone
in judicial considerations of methods of executions may be less clear than I have so far
made it out to be. Pain, as Scarry reminds us, is frequently used as a "symbolic substitute
for death" (ibid., 31). She argues that the world-destroying experience of physical pain is

Conclusion

In the United States, while law seems reconciled to state-imposed death, it is set on a quest to force the state to kill softly, gently, to impose no pain at all, or no more pain than is necessary.[121] That the law requires the state to kill in this manner seems, in one way, counterintuitive; it may precipitate one kind of crisis of legitimacy by distancing itself from the voices of victims and the demands of vengeance and, in so doing, by raising questions like those raised by the mother of a murder victim quoted in one of the epigraphs of this chapter—"Do they feel anything? Do they hurt? Is there any pain? Very humane compared to what they've done to our children. The torture they've put our kids through. I think sometimes it's too easy. They ought to feel something. If it's fire burning all the way through their body or whatever. There ought to be some little sense of pain to it."

Perhaps this strategy is less counterintuitive than it might otherwise seem. Alan Hyde, for example, argues that law's requirement that the state kill gently "follows a common pattern in which the humanistic, sentimentalized body in pain emerges as a site of empathy and identification" in the nineteenth and twentieth centuries.[122] Sentimentalizing the body of the condemned establishes, Hyde notes, a bridge between the criminal and the public. The criminal, no matter how horrific his deeds, is like us in his body's "amenability to feeling."[123] The concern that punishment not inflict physical pain and the empathy that it enables and expresses, Hyde observes, "lies behind the curious search in American legal history for painless methods of execution."[124] In an endlessly repeating ritual, he says, "electrocution, gas chambers, lethal injections are each introduced with tremendous fanfare as a painless form of death, until each is revealed to promote its own kind of suf-

---

an imaginative substitute for "what is unfeelable in death." Pain and death are "the most intense forms of negation, the purest expression of the anti-human, of annihilation, of total aversiveness, though one is an absence and the other a felt presence." In her view, then, when the courts speak about pain, they are neither eliding nor displacing the subject of death. They are speaking to, and about, it in one of the most powerful ways available to human language.

121. Abernathy, "The Methodology of Death."
122. Hyde, *Bodies of Law*, 192.
123. Ibid., 193.
124. Ibid., 194.

fering on the way to death."[125] Yet, as Hyde himself recognizes, execution marks the limits of empathy, reminding citizens of the ultimate disconnection between themselves and the condemned, a disconnection that seeks to operate at the moral level.[126]

Thus the search for painless death might be better understood as one way of keeping the simplifying, sentimental narratives of criminal and victim intact by not allowing those condemned to die to assume the status of victims of outmoded technologies of death, or as a response to one kind of crisis in legitimacy through another legitimation strategy.[127] Law imposes on sovereignty the requirement that no matter how heinous the crime, or how reprehensible the criminal, that we not do death as death has been done by those we punish. We give them a kinder, gentler death than they deserve to mark a boundary between the "civilized" and the "savage"[128] rather than to establish a connection between citizens and murderers. We kill gently not out of concern for the condemned but rather to vividly establish a hierarchy between the law-abiding and the lawless.[129]

The boundary-marking, hierarchy-establishing function of law's search for a technique of imposing death painlessly was put vividly on display recently in Justice Scalia's response to Justice Blackmun's dissent from a Supreme Court denial of certiorari in a death penalty case. In that dissent, Blackmun announced that he no longer would "tinker with the machinery of death"[130] and would, as a result, vote against the death penalty in all subsequent cases. Scalia responded by noting that while Blackmun had described "with poignancy the death of a con-

---

125. Ibid.

126. Ibid.

127. As Abernathy puts it, "[T]he shifts from public to private executions and toward more humane means of killing have been designed to comfort the punisher, not the condemned" ("The Methodology of Death," 423).

128. Peter Fitzpatrick, *The Mythology of Modern Law* (London: Routledge, 1992).

129. Or, we do so to reduce administrative inconveniences associated with continued use of methods of state killing not at the cutting edge of technologies for taking life. As Judge Harding noted when he called on the Florida legislature to authorize the use of lethal injection, "Florida death row inmates almost routinely challenge electrocution as a cruel and unusual punishment. . . . Such challenges consume an inordinate amount of the time and resources expended by inmates' counsel, State counsel, and judicial personnel. Furthermore, each time an execution is carried out, the courts wait in dread anticipation of some 'unforeseeable accident' that will set in motion a frenzy of inmate petitions and other filings" (*Provenzano,* 9 and 10).

130. *Callins v. Collins,* 510 U.S. 1141, 1145 (1994).

victed murderer by lethal injection,"[131] compared with what the condemned had done—"the murder of a man ripped by a bullet suddenly
and unexpectedly . . . left to bleed to death on the floor of a tavern—"[132]
death by lethal injection was "pretty desirable."[133] How enviable, Scalia
continued, "a quiet death by lethal injection compared with that!"[134]

We may not be able to know death, or comprehend its possibilities or
its horrors,[135] but where law requires the killing state to kill softly, it
restrains the state from fully and completely giving in to calls for
vengeance and, in so doing, seeks legitimacy in a not very veiled image of
the hand of punishment humanely applied. It may be death we are doing,
but it is a death whose savagery law insists it can, and will, control.

For the judges in *Campbell, Fierro,* and *Provenzano* close examination of the technologies of death deployed by the state takes the form of
an effort to prevent the erosion of the boundaries between the state's
violence and its extralegal counterpart. As Judge Shaw observed, "The
color photos of Davis depict a man who—for all appearances—was
brutally tortured to death by the citizens of Florida. . . . Each botched
execution cast[s] the entire criminal justice system of this state—including the courts—in ignominy."[136] The killing state depends on law both
to deploy and to mask power, to enable and to hide the violence on
which that state ultimately depends. Yet the fact that the state takes life,
and that it is everywhere a response to an imagined violence, generates
an anxious questioning within, and about, the ways state violence differs from the violence to which it is, at least in theory, opposed. The
effort to kill softly, gently, painlessly, humanely is one response to that
questioning, one way of trying to show that the state, though it comes
into the world born of physical violence, or the violent disruptions of
the existing order of things,[137] can transcend the violence of its origins.

As a response to this anxious questioning, the courts insist on
policing the technologies of death to ensure that sovereign power
responds to scientific progress, that ferocity gives way to bureaucracy,

131. Ibid., 1142.

132. Ibid.

133. Ibid.

134. Ibid.

135. Catherine Russell, *Narrative Mortality: Death, Closure, and New Wave Cinemas*
(Minneapolis: University of Minnesota Press, 1995).

136. *Provenzano,* 65.

137. Walter Benjamin, "Critique of Violence," in *Reflections: Essays, Aphorisms, and
Autobiographical Writing,* trans. Edmund Jephcott (New York: Schocken Books, 1986).

that it proceeds judiciously, using no more force than is absolutely necessary. State killing, guided by the restraining hand of law, in this view should be rational, purposive, and proportional; the violence to which it responds is, in contrast, imagined to be irrational, anomic, excessive. In the face of scientific "progress" in the technologies of death, the forms of legal procedure cannot condone archaic displays of sovereignty like those demanded by the survivors and families of the victims of the Oklahoma City bombing or like the botched execution of Pedro Medina. On this account the survival of state killing as an exercise of sovereign power depends on its being subject, even if against its will, to an unending search for technologies that in their ability to kill softly, gently, painlessly allow those who kill both to end life and, at the same time, believe themselves to be the guardians of a moral order that, in part, bases its claims to superiority in its condemnation of killing.

What the Law Must Not Hear: On Capital Punishment and the Voice of Pain

Timothy V. Kaufman-Osborn

"Legal interpretation takes place in a field of pain and death."[1] The law of the liberal state, Robert Cover observed, seeks to distance itself from the violence implicated in its very existence. To do so, to cite but one example, the law detaches the pronouncement of a death sentence from its imposition. Although less often noted, much the same end is achieved via the law's endorsement of a culturally specific construction of pain. That account, occluding its own historicity, renders pain radically solipsistic and so effectively unintelligible. To the extent that this antipolitical construction has also been embraced by the foes of specific methods of execution and capital punishment more generally, within the academy as well as within the courtroom, it compromises their ability to render pain visible and so contestable. To trouble this construction, I will suggest that pain might profitably be figured not as a brute unverifiable reality located exclusively within the hidden interior of the hurt body, but as a cultural artifact, indeed, as a sort of language. Doing so may render problematic the law's efforts to contain the harm it does by separating word from deed, sentence from execution; and that in turn may advance the goal sought by Cover, that is, to indicate how pain circulates throughout the entire legal order.

---

1. Robert Cover, "Violence and the Word," *Yale Law Journal* 95 (1986): 1601.

Modernist Pain

> [Pain] is not a *something,* but not a *nothing* either!
> —Ludwig Wittgenstein, *Philosophical Investigations*

In its modernist construction, pain is typically figured as a complex signal broadcast through the nervous system and carried from the site of
bodily harm to the brain. For political purposes, it is important to recall
that this is a historically specific conception. To see the point, one need
only consider Blaise Pascal's "Prayer to Ask God for the Good Use of
Sickness":

> Make me fully understand that the ills of the body are nothing else
> than the punishment and the encompassing symbol for the ills of
> the soul. O, Lord, let them be the remedy, by making me aware,
> through the pain that I feel, of the pain that I did not feel in my
> soul, deeply sick though it was and covered with sores. Because,
> Lord, the greatest sickness is insensibility. Let me feel this pain
> sharply, so that I can make whatever is left of my life a continual
> penance to wash away the offenses I have committed.[2]

On Pascal's Jansenist account, the body is conceived as a carnal enve-
lope imprisoning the soul, and the body's pain is a sign of the just punishment endured by that irremediably diseased soul in virtue of the primal sin of Adam and Eve. As such, pain is to be greeted with
resignation, but also with gratitude insofar as, and no doubt paradoxi-
cally to profane ears, it calls the sufferer to an awareness of the body's
ultimate insignificance. Alternatively, as intimated by the etymological
link joining the terms *excruciating* and *crucifixion,* Catholic pain is sometimes spiritualized via its sublimation within the narrative of the Passion and death of Christ. On either formulation, the unintelligibility of
the body's woes absent its theological construction is suggested by the
lack of any separate entry for the term *pain (peine)* in the Catholic *Dictionnaire de théologie,* published between 1935 and 1972. In that com-
pendium, discussion of what secular humanists would call *pain* is
found partly under the entry *mal* (evil, adversity) and partly under
Providence, thus suggesting the Catholic vacillation between, on the one

---

2. Blaise Pascal, quoted in David Morris, *The Culture of Pain* (Berkeley and Los
Angeles: University of California Press, 1991), 44.

hand, the formulation of pain as a foretaste of God's final retribution and, on the other hand, its formulation as a test of moral fortitude and hence as a token of eventual redemption.[3]

On this theological account, explains Ivan Illich, what was quite literally unthinkable was the belief that pain should or could be wholly eradicated through the intervention of any human agent, whether priest, politician, or physician. If pain is a mark of the corruption of nature, of which depraved humanity is undeniably a part, then it can no more be eliminated than can the human condition itself.[4] Not surprisingly, given this construction, throughout the eighteenth century and well into the nineteenth, European and American clergy played a major role in ministering to those in pain. Only after 1846, when a Boston dentist by the name of William Morton demonstrated that the vapor of diethyl ether could forestall the agonies of surgery, did the claims of physicians begin to supplant those of the clergy.[5] While the details of this conflict need not concern me, its results do. That we now think of pain as an unqualified evil, one that is to be entirely overcome, if at all possible, testifies to modern medicine's successful expropriation and colonization of this domain of experience.[6]

On the face of it, the modern medicalized construction of pain is a straightforward matter. This is a rationalized construction in the Weberian sense, that is, in the sense that its formulation in the language of modern science entails the withering away of the traditional moral and religious vocabularies that once folded pain within the more com-

---

3. Roselyne Rey, *The History of Pain* (Cambridge: Harvard University Press, 1995), 184.

4. Ivan Illich, *Medical Nemesis* (New York: Pantheon, 1976), 149.

5. See Martin Pernick, *A Calculus of Suffering* (New York: Columbia University Press, 1985).

6. My representation of modernist pain as an unmitigated evil to be wholly eradicated requires some qualification. It is only in recent decades that the medical profession has come to think of pain's amelioration as something akin to a categorical imperative. When anesthesia was first introduced, by way of contrast, it was not uncommon for physicians to resist its use in surgery either on the ground that the pain that accompanies and follows an operation is a functionally necessary constituent of the physiological processes of recuperation, or on the ground that such pain is a form of divine punishment for human depravity. Traces of this theological construction remain apparent in the discourse of those who represent the pain endured by AIDS patients as a punishment for sinful sexual conduct. Moreover, the colloquial expression "no pain, no gain" suggests that in certain contexts—e.g., athletic competitions and bodybuilding—pain is not figured as a purely aversive reality; and much the same is true of those who argue on behalf of "natural" childbirth.

prehensive category of suffering. To the biomedical researcher, pain is understood not as a manifestation of some disorder or malady stitched into the very seams of the cosmos, but as an aversive effect occasioned by changes in various etiological mechanisms, including sensory receptors, afferent neuronal relays, and spinal-cord, midbrain, or higher cortical modulating systems. Read as an indicator of nociception, that is, as a sign or symptom of injury or disease, modernist pain is to be professionally managed either by removing its cause or, failing that, by the administration of analgesia.

One might argue, as does Illich, that the resulting technological conception of pain evacuates it of all possible meaning:

> When cosmopolitan medical civilization colonizes any traditional culture, it transforms the experience of pain. The same nervous stimulation that I shall call "pain sensation" will result in a distinct experience, depending not only on personality but also on culture. This experience, as distinct from the painful sensation, implies a uniquely human performance called *suffering*. Medical civilization, however, tends to turn pain into a technical matter and thereby deprives suffering of its inherent personal meaning. Cultures are systems of meanings, cosmopolitan civilization a system of techniques. Culture makes pain tolerable by integrating it into a meaningful setting; cosmopolitan civilization detaches pain from any subjective or intersubjective context in order to annihilate it. Culture makes pain tolerable by interpreting its necessity; only pain perceived as curable is intolerable.[7]

Leaving aside the problematic distinction he draws here between the universal "painful sensation" and the culturally specific experience of it (to which I shall return later), and leaving aside his failure to recognize that modernist discourse does not so much evacuate pain of all sense, as narrow its range of meanings to those that conform to the imperatives of biomedical intelligibility, Illich is quite right to suggest that when this vocabulary no longer appears to be one among many possible candidates for making sense of pain, and when those who speak this language come to believe that, in doing so, they are disclosing incontestable *facts* about the body in pain, what was once an inher-

---

7. Illich, *Medical Nemesis*, 133–34.

ently contestable sense-making discourse is effectively naturalized and so depoliticized. "Living in a society that values anesthesia," he concludes, "both doctors and their potential clients are retrained to smother pain's intrinsic question mark."[8]

But is the modernist medical construction of pain as internally coherent as Illich's rhetoric intimates? Is it possible that this construction, no matter how successful at vanquishing its opponents, is nonetheless troubled by difficulties that can be publicly acknowledged only at the cost of calling into question the medical profession's self-representation? To indicate why this may be so, let me begin with a standard biomedical definition of pain. The International Association for the Study of Pain fixes the subject of its inquiry as follows: "Pain is an unpleasant sensory and emotional experience associated with actual or potential tissue damage or described in terms of such damage."[9] This definition, which is part of a more comprehensive attempt to formulate a standardized vocabulary for professional students of pain, represents a strategic attempt to negotiate some of its more vexing conundrums. Specifically, and as the phrase "actual or potential" intimates, this definition acknowledges that there is no necessary correlation between the extent of what the IASP calls "tissue damage" and the intensity or even the experience of pain. It is quite possible, for example, for someone to be in intense pain without displaying any tissue damage, just as it is possible for someone to display severe tissue damage and yet feel no pain.

In their oft-cited *Handbook of Pain Assessment*, Dennis Turk and Ronald Melzack commend the IASP on the grounds that its definition, precisely because it acknowledges the causal discontinuity between injury and pain, "underscores the inherent subjectivity of pain."[10] That subjectivity, they continue, is a function of pain's inaccessibility. While a physician may locate the cause of my pain (e.g., a wound) or its symptom (e.g., swelling), she cannot point to my pain per se (just as I cannot point to the color of a piece of paper); and, because pain can neither be identified with nor located neatly within any determinate embodied site, it would seem to follow that it must be something that resides in

---

8. Illich, *Medical Nemesis*, 143.

9. International Association for the Study of Pain, "Pain Terms: A List with Definitions and Notes on Usage," *Pain* 6 (1979): 249.

10. Dennis Turk and Ronald Melzack, *Handbook of Pain Assessment* (New York: Guilford, 1992), xi.

the ethereal and invisible domain of consciousness. Precisely because it is so located, any person's claim to be in pain is, strictly speaking, incorrigible in the sense that it cannot meaningfully be denied by another. (To see the point, consider the following exchange: You say, "I am in pain," to which I respond: "No, you are mistaken.")

But if indeed pain is radically solipsistic, as this exchange suggests, then it cannot help but pose awkward questions for those, like the members of the IASP, who are committed to its scientific analysis. For example, the absence of any isomorphic or linear causal relationship between bodily damage and pain mocks the hope, once entertained by medical researchers, of precisely mapping the pathways taken by neural impulses from the site of harm to the brain. Still more generally, it undermines medicine's confidence in its ability to identify a pathophysiological cause for every report of pain and so threatens to render some instances simply inexplicable. Tacitly acknowledging that the subjectivism of the definition they have endorsed cuts against their ability to articulate a scientific account of its operation, Turk and Melzack are quick to insist that, if inquirers are to "understand and adequately treat pain, we need to be able to measure it."[11] But this effort to recapture pain as a viable subject of positivist inquiry is quixotic at best, if only because different individuals who demonstrate the same sort of physical injury routinely offer radically incongruent statements concerning the intensity of their pain: "A number of cultural, economic, social, demographic, and environmental factors, along with the individual's personal history, situational factors, interpretation of the symptoms and resources, current psychological state, as well as physical pathology, all contribute to the response to the question 'How much does it hurt?'" Yet if that is so, that is, if there is "no simple thermometer that can objectively record how much pain an individual experiences,"[12] then that person's assessment of its intensity will tell us nothing about the "reality" of the harm suffered by the body and, as such, will take us nowhere in our efforts to get beyond pain's solipsism.

Some biomedical researchers have responded to this dilemma, Turk and Melzack concede, by arguing on behalf of a strict behaviorist conception of pain: "In an effort to avoid the problems inherent in self-reports of pain severity, some investigators and many clinicians suggest that the report of pain should be ignored because it is a symptom

11. Turk and Melzack, *Handbook of Pain Assessment*, xi.
12. Turk and Melzack, *Handbook of Pain Assessment*, xi, 5

rather than an objective sign that is believed to be more reliable and valid."[13] Persons in pain, adherents of this conception note, typically display a range of observable behaviors (e.g., moaning, limping, wincing, etc.). So as to avoid the puzzles encountered by formulations that read such conduct as an untrustworthy sign of pain that is itself inaccessible and unverifiable, the behaviorist account denies the privilege of reality to that which cannot be visibly confirmed and so concludes that such conduct *is* one's pain. From this conclusion, it follows that operant conditioning that successfully eliminates these learned behaviors will, by definition, rid the sufferer of his or her pain. However, and leaving aside the problem posed by the cross-cultural variability of conventional pain behaviors, it is all too easy to imagine a situation in which all of the observable indicators are present without a person actually being in pain (as in a theatrical performance). And, if that is so, then the presence of pain behavior cannot be equated *with* the experience of pain per se, although it is often identified *by* such behaviors.[14] In sum, whereas I can never be wrong when I claim that *I* am in pain, I can readily be in error when I make the same claim about another.

Caught between their endorsement of a subjectivist definition of pain and their objectivist requirement that it be a measurable public reality, Turk and Melzack seek to effect an epistemological compromise. In the last analysis, they concede, "anything that can be determined about the intensity of an individual's pain is based on what the patient verbally or nonverbally communicates about his or her subjective experience."[15] However, they go on, one can offset the problematic implications of this reliance on the idiosyncratic by asking sufferers to quantify their pain, that is, to rank it on a scale of zero to ten. Yet this compromise is ultimately unsatisfactory, first, because the privatism of the scaling systems generated by diverse individuals is inconsistent with the very concept of measurement, and, second, because its quantitative reductionism cannot capture the qualitative dimensions that experientially distinguish this pain from that. True, one might respond to this latter deficiency by developing, as does the McGill-Melzack Pain Questionnaire,[16] a series of terms that seek to tap into pain's qualitative

13. Turk and Melzack, *Handbook of Pain Assessment*, 6–7.

14. On this point, see Dennis Turk and Herta Flor, "Pain > Pain Behaviors: The Utility and Limitations of the Pain Behavior Construct," *Pain* 31 (1987): 277–95.

15. Turk and Melzack, *Handbook of Pain Assessment*, 5.

16. Ronald Melzack, "The McGill Pain Questionnaire: Major Properties and Scoring Methods," *Pain* 1 (1975): 277–99.

dimensions (e.g., "burning," "pinching," "gnawing," etc.). But, so long as one cannot determine the fidelity of these terms to the reality they are said to represent, except via the testimony of the sufferer, this strategy cannot satisfy the demands of a positivist epistemology that must presuppose the cognitive availability of a world of intersubjectively verifiable objects. If pain is ultimately whatever the individual sufferer says it is, and if it routinely frustrates efforts to delineate its operation in the terms of linear causality, then the possibility of rendering it a fit object of biomedical inquiry is compromised, perhaps irreparably. "Pain," concludes Arthur Kleinman, "eludes the [medical] discipline's organized explanatory systems as much as it escapes the diagnostic net of biomedical categories."[17]

Rebuttable Pain

> An execution is not a complex verbal event.
>
> —Karl Mayer

What happens when the dilemmas inherent within the modernist construction of pain are imported within the domain of law, and, more particularly, what happens when such pain becomes a contested issue within the context of a lawful execution? Before moving directly to these questions, it is important to note that just as the construction of pain is historically and culturally specific, so too is the construction of its relationship to capital punishment. To see the point, one need only recall the familiar account, offered by Foucault in *Discipline and Punish*, of the execution of the attempted regicide Damiens in 1757.[18] That highly ritualized spectacle represented an awesome reaffirmation of compromised sovereign power. The success of that reaffirmation, whose purpose was to purge the body politic of its infected organ and thereby heal its remainder, demanded maximal intensification of the condemned's pain. Damiens's agony is rendered meaningful via its incorporation within a cosmological narrative concerning the status of the monarch as the inviolable head of the interdependent body politic,

---

17. Arthur Kleinman, "Pain and Resistance: The Delegitimation and Relegitimation of Local Worlds," in *Pain as Human Experience: An Anthropological Perspective*, ed. Mary-Jo DelVecchio Good et al. (Berkeley and Los Angeles: University of California Press, 1992), 170.

18. Michel Foucault, *Discipline and Punish*, trans. Alan Sheridan (New York: Vintage, 1979), 3–6.

which in turn references the king's standing as God's agent on earth. Propelled by that narrative, the pain of Damiens ramifies beyond the finite limits of his body, moving in one direction toward the temporal political order he sought to dismember, and in the other toward the eternal agonies his soul is certain to suffer in hell. The claims of the former are incarnated in the persons of the magistrate and the executioner, while the claims of the latter are embodied in the person of the priest. Neither articulates the construction of pain figured in the person of the physician.

The medicalization of pain is one of the distinguishing features of modern executions. In his comparative account of two state-sponsored killings in New York, the first in 1825 and the second in 1892, Michael Madow notes that questions that figured centrally in the latter were strikingly absent in the former. When James Reynolds was publicly hanged in New York City in 1825, the report offered by the *Commercial Advertiser* ended with this statement: "The cap was then drawn over his eyes and at a quarter before one o'clock while he was earnestly crying to God for pardon the drop fell and he was launched into eternity." As Madow notes, "what is interesting here is what was left *unreported*. Did Reynolds' neck vertebrae snap, killing him quickly? Or did he die a slow death by strangulation? Did he struggle? Did he suffer? We are not told . . . It was Reynold's soul, not his body, that claimed the narrative's center."[19] By way of contrast, when Charles McElvaine was privately electrocuted at Sing Sing some sixty-six years later, physicians, not clergy members, dominated the scene, and the questions posed by journalists assembled outside the penitentiary all presupposed this event's medicalized construction: "Exactly when did McElvaine die? When did he lose consciousness? Did he feel any pain? Was there any burning of the flesh?"[20]

On this account, the question of McElvaine's soul is eclipsed by that of his body; and, although no doubt the break from earlier sensibilities is not entire, his body is itself understood as something akin to the unambiguously demarcated biomechanical entity that appears self-evidently real to us today. This body's sense is derived not from the comprehensive domains of political or cosmological significance from which it has now been effectively amputated, but from its relationship

---

19. Michael Madow, "Forbidden Spectacle: Executions, the Public, and the Press in Nineteenth Century America," *Buffalo Law Review* 43 (1995): 486.

20. Madow, "Forbidden Spectacle," 486.

to the individual person who bears this proper name. Over the course of the nineteenth century, argues Alan Hyde, "a distinctively modern body takes shape in legal and popular culture, a body that represents an individuated, human spirit that is the person inside it, a person that controls that body but is not identical to it."[21] On this neo-Cartesian understanding, it is the person not the body that commits crime, for the body cannot be ascribed any autonomous legal agency. Hence, when the state incarcerates that body, its aim is to deprive the person housed within, the fictive subject of law's imperatives, of its rights. Because that legal subject is not itself regarded as a material entity, as is the body, when the law punishes, its aim cannot be the infliction of pain per se. Accordingly, when any given punishment does in fact cause pain, modern liberal law confronts a dilemma it is ill equipped to resolve. That dilemma is all the more pressing when the question of pain arises in the context of a death sentence. There, the aim of law is still to employ the palpable body as a means to the deprivation of abstract rights, and in this sense that body is incidental to the law's ultimate objective. What complicates this project, of course, is capital punishment's status as the last remaining penalty that accomplishes its purpose via the deliberate and direct infliction of harm upon the body. That imperative cannot help but coexist uneasily with the self-understanding of a liberal state, which, throughout the nineteenth and twentieth centuries, has been ever more given to humanitarian pieties, and so ever more pressed by its own discourse to embrace the sentimental ideal of a death that involves no pain.

The state's ability to occlude the suffering caused by this most dramatic manifestation of its monopolization of the means of violence is enhanced by the medicalized representation of pain as an effect caused by pathophysiological injury and localized within the body's invisible confines. Just as the law teaches us to accept as real certain forms of violence, but to dismiss others (consider, e.g., the unproblematic status of domestic violence until recently), so too does a medicalized conception of pain encourage us to acknowledge certain forms of suffering, but to discount others. Most obviously, this conception will not call our attention to suffering that has no identifiable physiological cause (consider, e.g., the terror of knowing the precise moment when one is scheduled

---

21. Alan Hyde, *Bodies of Law* (Princeton, N.J.: Princeton University Press, 1997), 9.

to die). Especially when joined to claims about its inherent subjectivity, which invite persons to doubt the reality of others' suffering, the confinement of pain to the unseen interior of the body severs the relational connections, truncates the lines of implication, that were far more apparent when "individuals" were understood as organs of a larger body politic and when the pain suffered by such organs was saturated with cosmological import. Accompanied by the removal of executions to the interior of penitentiaries, the transformation of executioners into impersonal bureaucratic officials, and the adoption of execution methods that leave the condemned body unmarked, the contemporary construction of pain contributes to the state's effort to reduce the likelihood that executions will generate disconcerting questions about the justice or legitimacy of the political order that mandates this punishment.

But matters are rarely if ever quite this simple. If, as I suggested in the previous section, the biomedical construction of pain is internally conflicted, do traces of that trouble sometimes surface within the law? More pointedly, what happens when an execution is bungled in a way that compels the law to confront the question of pain? To answer these questions, and to do so in a way that indicates how uncritical adoption of the modernist account of pain compromises the efforts of those who seek to render it conspicuous, in the remainder of this section, I will explore the execution of Allen Lee Davis as well as the Florida Supreme Court case in which the corpse of Davis figured centrally.

Allen Lee Davis, nicknamed "Tiny," was convicted on three counts of first-degree murder in 1983 and sentenced to die; his victims included Nancy Weiler, the pregnant wife of a Westinghouse executive, and their two daughters, Kristine, age nine, and Katherine, age five. Some fifteen years later, concerned about the ability of its seventy-four-year-old wooden electric chair to withstand Davis's 350 pounds, the state of Florida elected to build a new frame, although most of the original wiring system was retained. The following June, Governor Jeb Bush signed his first two death warrants, one for Davis and another for Thomas Provenzano, who was convicted in the shooting death of an Orange County bailiff during a hearing on a disorderly conduct charge. On July 8, 1999, just after 7:00 A.M., Davis was strapped into Florida's electric chair and, at 7:09 A.M., a private citizen who was paid $150 and whose identity was hidden by a hood threw a switch that released an initial fifteen-hundred-volt charge for 10 seconds, followed by a second jolt of six hundred volts for 4.5 seconds, and, finally, another fifteen-hundred-volt blast for 10 seconds. Davis, also hooded, was pronounced dead at 7:15.

Although no recent execution employing "Old Sparky" has gone without comment, Florida's killing of Davis provoked a furor. Why it did so is indicated in the following account offered by the *St. Petersburg Times:*

> Two muffled screams were heard from Davis just before the executioner threw the switch. Davis jolted back into the chair and clenched his fist, a sight common to Florida executions. Blood appeared to pour from the mouth and ooze from the chest of Allen Lee "Tiny"' Davis as he was hit with 2,300 [sic] volts. By the time Davis was pronounced dead at 7:15 A.M., the blood from his mouth had poured out onto the collar of his white shirt, and the blood on his chest had spread to about the size of a dinner plate, even seeping through the buckle holds on the leather chest strap holding him to the chair. The heavy bleeding was believed to be a first for 44 modern Florida executions.[22]

At a press conference immediately following Davis's execution, a spokesperson for Governor Bush, Cory Tilley, announced to the assembled reporters that "nothing went wrong. The chair functioned as it was designed to function and we're comfortable that that worked."[23] However, speaking for the Department of Corrections, Eugene Morris confessed that "the blood is not normal. . . . I've witnessed 15 and I've never seen blood."[24] Uncertain what to make of these conflicting accounts, just eleven hours after Davis was pronounced dead, the Florida Supreme Court stayed the execution of Provenzano, who had been scheduled to die the following morning.

Because idiosyncratic human bodies are rarely as predictable as the law wishes them to be, executions always harbor the potential to unsettle the conventional understandings that otherwise stabilize the law's routinized authority. What rendered this particular event extraordinary, of course, was the blood that violated accustomed sensibili-

---

22. "Davis Execution Turns Bloody," *St. Petersburg Times,* July 8, 1999, 1.
23. "Davis Execution Turns Bloody," 1.
24. "Bloody Execution Leads to Stay for Second Inmate," *St. Petersburg Times,* July 9, 1999, 1.

ties concerning what belongs inside the body and what belongs on its outside. That crimson stream eluded the law's effort to contain the meaning of this execution, and it did so by transforming the corpse of Allen Davis into an unsettling question mark. Did he suffer? If so, how much, for how long, and why? Pain, as I indicated in the previous section, is not self-announcing; it requires some mode of articulation in order to make its appearance in the public world. But the import of that which is legible, in this instance, the blood of Allen Davis, is never self-evident. As such, it is subject to differential interpretation and therefore, at least potentially, a matter of political contest.

The terminus of this particular contest was announced by the Florida Supreme Court when, on September 24, 1999, it ruled that employment of the electric chair is not unconstitutional. Of limited interest to me is the specifically legal reasoning that drew the court, by a vote of four to three, to this conclusion. Suffice it to say that, citing *Gregg v. Georgia*, 428 U.S. 153 (1976) and *Louisiana ex rel. Francis v. Resweber*, 329 U.S. 459 (1947), the court argued that "in order for a punishment to constitute cruel or unusual punishment, it must involve 'torture or a lingering death' or the infliction of 'unnecessary and wanton pain'";[25] because the record, on the court's account, demonstrated that Davis died immediately and painlessly, execution by electrocution does not offend either of these tests. Of greater interest to me are the eight findings of fact that were generated by the circuit court as a result of its evidentiary hearing and then adopted by the majority as the basis for its decision. Collectively, these findings enunciate the law's effort to navigate the troubling uncertainty of Davis's bloodstained shirt and, more specifically, its status as a possible trace of the pain that, in the last analysis, it will deny. Slightly abridged, those findings are as follows:

1. During the execution of Allen Lee Davis, the electric chair functioned as it was intended to function.
2. The cycles of voltage and amperage applied in the execution of Allen Lee Davis did not deviate from the execution protocol which was previously approved by the Florida Supreme Court.
3. The death of Allen Lee Davis did not result from asphyxiation caused by the mouth strap.

25. *Provenzano v. Moore*, Case No. 95, 973, Corrected Opinion (September 24, 1999), Supreme Court of Florida.

4. Allen Lee Davis did not suffer any conscious pain while being electrocuted in Florida's electric chair. Rather, he suffered instantaneous and painless death once the current was applied to him.

5. The nose bleed incurred by Allen Lee Davis began *before* the electrical current was applied to him, and was not caused whatsoever by the application of electrical current to Davis.

6. The post-execution photographs of Allen Lee Davis indicate that the straps used to restrain Davis's body, specifically, the mouth strap and chin strap, may have caused Davis to suffer some discomfort. However, the straps did not cause him to suffer unnecessary and wanton pain, and the mouth strap was not a part of the electrical operation of the electric chair.

7. The use of a mouth strap to secure an inmate's head to the electric chair may be desirable, however, a smaller and/or redesigned mouth strap could accomplish the same purpose without raising the same issue involved here.

8. Execution inherently involves fear, and it may involve some degree of pain. That pain may include pain associated with affixing straps around the head and body to secure the head and body [to] the electric chair. However, any pain associated therewith is necessary to ensure that the integrity of the execution process is maintained.[26]

To ears untutored in the law, much like the naive eyes that first saw the video of Rodney King's beating at the hands of the Los Angeles police department, the initial accounts of Davis's execution most certainly testified to the reality of a body in torment. But, the court explains, after applying a method of analysis that in certain respects is very much like that employed by the defense attorneys who disaggregated the King footage into so many freeze-frame fragments, what the ears believe they hear and the eyes think they see are often poor guides to what the law knows about pain.

The initial strategy adopted by the circuit court to dispel the political awkwardness occasioned by Davis's blood consists of its effort to specify that fluid's exact point of origin and, in so doing, to check its capacity to seep into areas where the law might find its meaning more

26. *Provenzano v. Moore*, 2–3.

difficult to contain. Contrary to reports generated by eyewitnesses to Davis's execution, some of whom maintained that blood oozed from his mouth and/or his chest, autopsy reports introduced during the evidentiary hearing indicated that its sole source was his nose. Moreover, witnesses for the state testified, Davis was predisposed to nosebleeds because, for some time, he had been taking blood-thinning drugs, including aspirin and Motrin, as a remedy for the pain caused by severe osteoarthritis. The court thereby offers a scientifically intelligible account for Davis's nosebleed, one that tacitly references the medical profession's status as minister to the body's woes and, by implication, the state's solicitude prior to his execution. Deflecting attention from the extraordinary circumstances of its production, this mundane explanation domesticates what might otherwise be taken as a disturbing signifier of barbarous violence.

Yet those circumstances cannot be denied altogether, and so, as a complement to its spatial localization, the circuit court seeks to temporally circumscribe Davis's blood as well. By emphatically insisting that the nosebleed "began *before* the electrical current was applied to him," the court implies that it should not be understood as an immanent part of the execution proper. The relevant Florida statute (section 922.10) mandates that "a death sentence shall be executed by electrocution." Therefore, strictly speaking, a consideration of Davis's nosebleed is irrelevant to an assessment of this method's constitutionality. By rendering legally inconsequential everything that occurs prior to the moment when the switch is finally thrown, the law effectively distances itself from the injury that Davis's blood so insistently proclaims. Having done so, the state can then concede that "the mouth strap and chin strap may have caused Davis to suffer some discomfort" (although the term "may" suggests the epistemological uncertainty of even that conclusion, and the term "discomfort" represents Davis's suffering as a minor irritation at best), without worrying that this acknowledgment will compromise its affirmation of this way of killing.

However, this strategy of disaggregating the act of killing into those components that are constitutionally salient and those that are not is not itself free of risk. If the blood in question "was not caused whatsoever by the application of electrical current to Davis" (does not the court protest too much?), then what was its cause? As the court acknowledges, the broad leather strap circling the lower portion of Davis's head, covering his mouth, pushing up hard against his nostrils, buckled tightly behind his head, is the obvious culprit. But does that suggest, as those in dissent do, that the screams heard by several witnesses just prior to the first jolt of electricity were so many inarticulate protests against the onset of asphyxiation? And if that is so, should we conclude that deprivation of oxygen was a contributing cause of Davis's death? And if that is so, did the conduct of this execution violate the terms of the statute that the state so carefully cited in its own defense just a moment ago? Should we determine that, because not one but two causes of death were involved, the execution of Allen Lee Davis was at least in part an act of lawless violence? To nip this series of questions in the bud, the circuit court asserts that "the mouth strap was not a part of the electrical operation of the electric chair." Doing so, and consistent with its initial strategy, it defines this apparatus in a way such that the specific part that may have occasioned some "discomfort" is adventitious to the act of killing and, as such, irrelevant to the execution of a lawful sentence by electrocution. (However, if the strap is indeed irrelevant in this sense, it is not clear why this court of law deems it appropriate to recommend specific technical modifications in its design.) Perhaps sensing that this semantic tactic is not altogether persuasive, and ignoring considerable contrary evidence introduced at the evidentiary hearing, the court simply declares as a categorical fact that "the death of Allen Lee Davis did not result from asphyxiation caused by the mouth strap."

What is almost entirely missing from the circuit court's findings of fact is any representation of Davis as what Alan Hyde calls a "sympathetic body,"[27] that is, the sort of body that is dangerous to the law precisely because it invites intersubjective identification. Perhaps that sort of body makes an oblique appearance when, in the eighth finding, we are told that "execution inherently involves fear." But, given that such fear is not ascribed to Davis in particular, and given that all of the other findings reduce him either to the status of an abstract legal person (the figure that appears whenever the name "Allen Lee Davis" is invoked) or to a mindless corporeal container that bears no essential connection to the autonomous subject housed within (the figure that appears whenever the term "body" is invoked), his capacity to distract from the genuinely significant constitutional question is radically constrained: "While there has been much said about the Davis execution because of

27. Hyde, *Bodies of Law*, 199.

the blood which dripped from the inmate's nostril during this process," notes an impatient Justice Quince in his concurring opinion, "the real question here is whether or not the use of electrocution violates the 'evolving standards of decency' espoused by the U.S. Supreme Court."[28]

The task for the dissenters on the Florida Supreme Court is to fashion such a sympathetic body or, rather, to stitch together Davis's body and mind so as to fashion an embodied person, and to do so in a way that makes his pain palpably real. Here, too, my interest is not in the specifically legal arguments that generate the conclusion that electrocution, because it causes undue pain and unnecessary mutilation, violates the cruel and unusual punishment clauses of the Florida and U.S. constitutions. Rather, my aim is to explore the strategies that are deployed in an effort to render plausible the contention, advanced by Justice Shaw in the most extensive of the three dissenting opinions, that Allen Lee Davis, "for all appearances, was brutally tortured to death by the citizens of Florida."[29] The foremost of these strategies consists of an effort to present the visual and auditory clues afforded by Davis before and after the administration of electrical current as incontestable indicia of pain. That effort proves ultimately unsuccessful, I will suggest, because the arguments of electrocution's opponents are bedeviled by a modernist conception of pain, one that vacillates indeterminately between equally unpersuasive subjectivist and objectivist accounts of its nature.

Shaw's initial effort to make Davis's pain real involves ascribing to him the voice of an autonomous subject who, in speaking, seeks to make public a truth that is otherwise hidden within his body's interior: "After Davis' airflow had been blocked by the mouth-strap, the face-mask, and his own blood, Davis made several sounds under the face-mask which were described variously as muffled screams, moans, or yells, as if he were attempting to get the guards' attention."[30] Bolstered by the testimony of a forensic pathologist who, on the basis of an independent autopsy, concluded that death was at least partly caused by asphyxiation, Shaw attempts to ascribe to Davis a deliberate intent, specifically, to request relief from the agony of suffocation. But, as his "as if" reveals, there is no way to overcome the speculative nature of

---

28. *Provenzano v. Moore*, 17.
29. *Provenzano v. Moore*, 65.
30. *Provenzano v. Moore*, 49.

this conjecture and so to adduce this evidence as indubitable proof of Davis's pain. Shaw seeks to overcome this epistemological lacuna by citing in rapid succession testimony from four eyewitnesses to the execution. None, however, is able to provide Shaw the certainty he requires: one, for example, "heard what sounded like two screams from Davis," while another "heard two muffled sounds from Davis, which sounded like Davis was trying to say something."[31] Was Davis, as this second witness suggests, attempting to give his pain intelligible linguistic form, say, in the form a call *for* help? Or, as the first witness appears to imply, was Davis reduced to the status of a brute body that could do no more than cry out *in* pain? Or, was John McNeill, utility supervisor at the Florida State Prison, closer to the mark when he testified that Davis "didn't make any sounds that wasn't normal. . . . He grunted then, all I heard, a grunt"?[32]

Given the modernist construction of pain, our perplexity in the face of these questions cannot help but remain unresolved. If Davis was in pain, just how severe was it? Given pain's resistance to objective measurement, unlike determination of the precise number of volts that coursed through his body, we cannot say. Indeed, are we sure that Davis, prior to the administration of electricity, endured *any* pain? Even if we concede that the indeterminate noises issuing from Davis's body signified his perception of suffering, given the absence of any necessary correlation between bodily harm and the experience of pain, is it not possible that the hurt Shaw thinks Davis sought to express had *no* pathophysiological cause, but instead was purely psychological in origin? And if that is so, then might we be tempted to say either that its cause was psychosomatic and so, from a biomechanical perspective, not quite real or, adding insult to alleged injury, that Davis was in some sense implicated in or even responsible for the production of his own pain? In sum, the attempt to treat Davis *as if* he were a conscious subject seeking to give voice to his suffering founders on the shoals of a solipsistic construction of pain that leaves us forever in doubt as to its reality. Not surprisingly, the court's majority exploits such skepticism in order to bolster its contention that Davis experienced no pain and, by implication, that the law is not an accomplice to torture.

Much the same sort of skepticism vitiates the second strategy deployed by those in dissent. Here, rather than seeking to ascribe a

---

31. *Provenzano v. Moore,* 49–50.
32. *Initial Brief of Petitioners,* Case Nos. 95, 959, 95, 973 (filed with the Supreme Court of Florida, August 8, 1999), 16.

voice to Davis, his mute body is read for visual signs of its suffering. Crucial to this effort are the postexecution photographs that Justice Shaw appends to his opinion and then posts on the website of the state's highest court (see photographs following page 90). Such evidence, Shaw wants to believe, precisely because it is *not* a matter of discursive construction, precisely because it is not compromised by the ambiguities of language, will surely speak for itself:

> The color photos taken by DOC [Department of Corrections] show a ghastly post-execution scene: Davis is wearing a white shirt and dark pants and is restrained in the wooden chair by thick leather straps placed across his arms, legs, torso, and mouth; the electrical head-piece is attached to the top of his head with a leather strap that turns under his chin; a sponge placed under the head-piece obscures the entire top portion of his head down to his eyebrows; because of the width of the mouth-strap, only a small portion of Davis' face is visible above the mouth-strap and below the sponge, and that portion is bright purple and scrunched tightly upwards; his eyes are clenched shut and his nose is pushed so severely upward that it is barely visible above the mouth-strap; although the exterior openings of Davis' nostrils are partially visible, it appears as though the interior openings may be covered by the mouth-strap; a stream of blood pours from his nostrils, flows over the wide leather mouth-strap, runs down his neck and chest, and forms a bright red pool (approximately eight by twelve inches) on his white shirt.[33]

Although certainly powerful, *pace* Shaw, this visual evidence does not in fact speak for itself.[34] Were it to do so, then any reading of these photographs, including that offered by Shaw, would be superfluous and so

---

33. *Provenzano v. Moore*, 51–52.

34. Granted, these photographs offer a different sort of testimony than do Shaw's words, if only because human eyes simultaneously grasp the coexistent parts of the whole that is offered by a visual representation, whereas language unfolds its synthetic meanings in time as each word gives way to the next. Whether intended or not, Shaw's prose attempts to mimic the visceral immediacy of these photographs through the breathlessness of this remarkable sentence, an effect created by the use of semi-colons wherever a period might introduce a more emphatic break. If only in part, Shaw's rhetoric thereby counters the majority's disaggregation of the extended performance that is the execution of Allen Lee Davis, its breaking of that complex event into so many discrete units of space and time, each of which can be rendered unproblematic in the eyes of the law.

he would find it unnecessary to affirm, as he does in the sentence immediately following, that "[t]he scene is unquestionably violent."[35] What Shaw presents as a transparent reproduction in words of what human eyes cannot help but see is better understood as a sort of performative utterance, one that participates in constructing the reality it claims to describe. That this reality can be fashioned otherwise is indicated, most obviously, by the majority's quite different reading. Whereas Shaw seeks to transpose the violence he finds in this postexecution scene backward in time so that it infects the entire event from start to finish, the majority has no difficulty concluding that whatever signs of "violence" appear here are "accidental" and, as such, do not call into question the essential lawfulness of death by electrocution.

Similar difficulties compromise the various forms of biomechanical evidence that are adduced in order to certify the reality of Davis's status as a body in pain. That evidence is problematic because, in addition to being hidden behind an opaque wall of flesh, its relevance to Davis can only be inferred. For example, the brief filed with the Florida Supreme Court by Provenzano's attorneys includes testimony from John Wikswo, who specializes in biological physics, biomedical engineering, and electrophysiology, and Donald Price, who wrote two chapters of *The Handbook of Pain Assessment*, cited above. "It may be possible," Wikswo contends, "for an inmate to maintain consciousness for 15 to 30 seconds into the execution."[36] During this period, he concludes, the condemned "will" experience multiple forms of pain as skeletal muscles tetanize, as pain centers in the brain are directly stimulated, as respiratory muscles are paralyzed, and as carbon dioxide levels rise rapidly in the blood, producing a sensation akin to that of suffocation. The more circumspect Dr. Price, however, is obliged to concede that, although medical science can offer an account of the "effect of electricity on biological tissue" as well as an account of "what physiological reactions are likely to occur as a result," it cannot in the last analysis do more than affirm that Davis "almost certainly experienced intense or severe pain during his judicial electrocution."[37] Once again, the absence of any necessary connection between physiological injury and the experience of pain saps the capacity to declare what otherwise seems so patently true.

35. *Provenzano v. Moore*, 52.
36. *Initial Brief of Petitioners*, 53.
37. *Initial Brief of Petitioners*, 43–44.

The electrocution of Allen Lee Davis

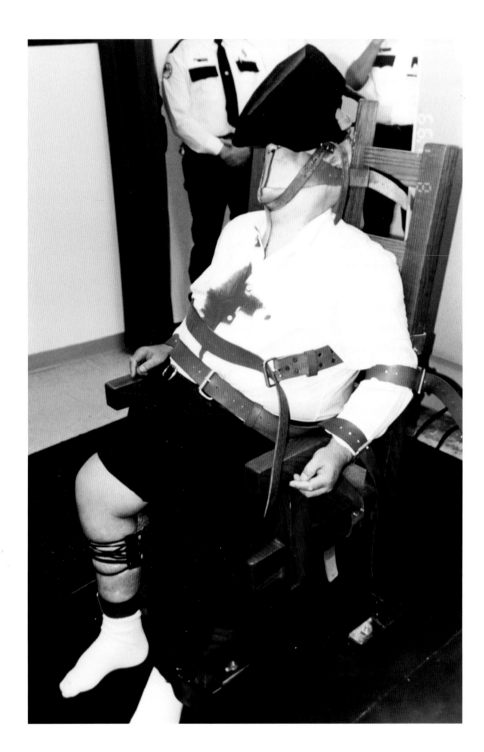

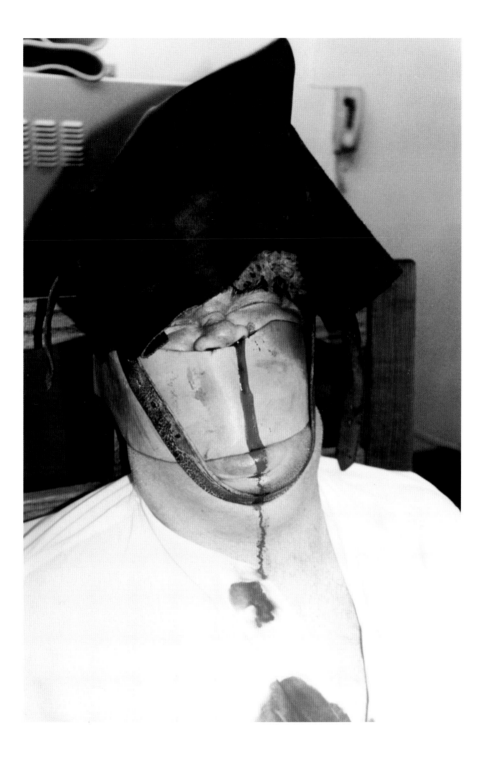

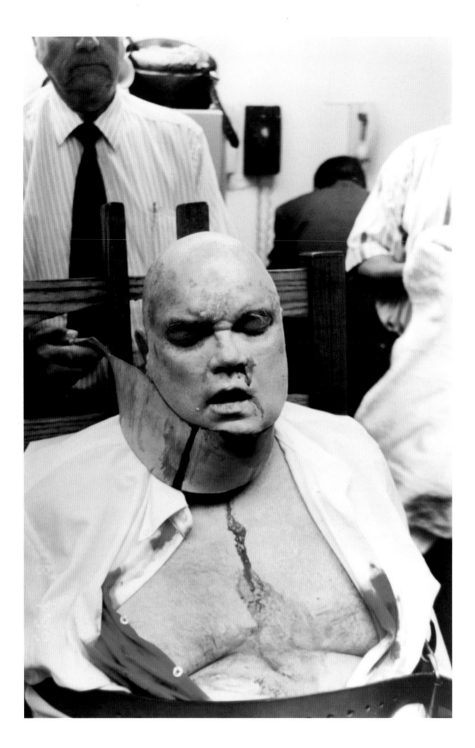

Eager to say something more definitive about Davis's suffering, Price shifts from invisible interior mechanisms to observable external indicators. "The behaviors that have been witnessed" on the part of the condemned during judicial electrocutions "are in many cases classic signs of pain in human beings, particularly given the context in which these behaviors are displayed. People moan, gasp for air, move their head from side to side and scream. Normally those behaviors are indicative of pain and even severe pain."[38] But Price's acknowledgment that the meaning of such behavior is not self-evident, that its import is contingent on an interpretation of the context within which it occurs, is precisely what denies him the ability to make the sort of emphatic claim that Justice Shaw requires. "People moan in their sleep," continues Price. "You wouldn't say that is pain; but if they are sitting in the electric chair and moaning, then it is much easier to infer the existence of pain."[39] Once again, this time from a behaviorist perspective, grasping the pain of another proves infernally elusive; its existence may be postulated on the basis of conduct and context, but its reality can never be affirmed beyond the shadow of a doubt.

The dilemma encountered in the effort to make Davis's pain real through an appeal to behavioral indicators takes a final ironic twist when his body is examined as a preface to formal certification of death. In what might appear to be a damning admission, several witnesses to the execution testified that Davis's chest dilated one or two times after the current was shut off for the final time. Those movements, hypothesized Steve Wellhausen, an employee of the prison, looked like someone "flexing their chest muscles or contracting their chest muscles."[40] If these movements can be construed as efforts at respiration rather than as reflex responses, then that would indicate that brain stem activity was still present (which is not altogether implausible since the human skull partly insulates the brain from electrical current and so may prevent it from causing instantaneous unconsciousness). Moreover, if, as some witnesses contended, Davis continued to bleed (as opposed to simply dripping residual blood from his nasal cavities) at the close of the execution, that would indicate that his heart was still beating. And if his brain and heart were still functioning, then it is possible that Davis retained some measure of consciousness and so was capable of

---

38. *Initial Brief of Petitioners,* 40.
39. *Initial Brief of Petitioners,* 40.
40. *Initial Brief of Petitioners,* 21–22.

experiencing pain even after the third jolt was completed. But if that was so, then how are we to explain the absence of any sort of aversive behavior on Davis's part during the intervals separating those three shocks? Surely, that indicates that he was not in pain. Or does it, given that electrical blasts of this magnitude stimulate each muscle to full contraction and so, in all likelihood, prevent the condemned from crying out or even moving when the current is temporarily stopped? In short, from the law's standpoint, one of the unanticipated virtues of electrocution as a method of execution, much like the anesthesia that renders unconscious those sentenced to die by lethal injection, may be its ability to suppress the behavioral evidence that might otherwise cause us to fret about a body in pain.

Given that it is possible to exhibit severe bodily damage and yet not be in pain, and given that it is possible to manifest all of the conventional signs of pain and yet not be in pain, the dissenters' invocation of various forms of behavioral evidence proves no more conclusive, no more immune to skeptical dismissal, than does the evidence teased from Davis's "voice." And, indeed, when all is said and done, perhaps Davis was simply faking it; or, less cruelly, perhaps what bleeding heart liberals take to be unequivocal indicators of pain are nothing more than muscular contractions caused by the application of intense electrical current. Are these speculations morally repugnant? Perhaps. But they may also be essential to the integrity of a legal order that must deafen itself to the pain it cannot in good conscience justify. Only that, I assume, can explain the Fourth Circuit's callous assertion, in a case dealing with the gas chamber, that "graphic descriptions of the death throes of inmates executed by gas are full of prose calculated to invoke sympathy, but insufficient to demonstrate that execution by the administration of gas involves the wanton and unnecessary infliction of pain."[41]

Political Pain

> I have given a name to my pain and call it "dog."
> —Friedrich Nietzsche, "The Gay Science"

The appeal to pain, construed in modernist terms, cannot furnish significant leverage to those who would challenge capital punishment on

---

41. *Hunt v. Nuth,* 57 F.3d 1327 (4th Cir. 1995): 1337–38.

the grounds that it inflicts what students of constitutional law call "wanton" or "unnecessary" pain.[42] In light of that conclusion, in this final section, more suggestively than conclusively, I want to indicate how we might begin to temper the incapacities of this construction by reconsidering the relationship between pain and language; and to do that I will turn to what I take to be the most seductive contemporary meditation on this question, Elaine Scarry's *The Body in Pain*. On the one hand, her account of this relationship is to be resisted. By endowing pain with a terrifying capacity to destroy all language, she renders it fundamentally incontestable and so not merely apolitical but even antipolitical. On the other hand, her account opens up political possibilities she herself does not recognize, and it does so by indicating how pain is sometimes transformed into language and, more specifically, the language of power.

Much of Scarry's analysis turns on what might be characterized as a hyperbolic rendering of the subjectivist account of pain. That conception, recall, presupposes pain's essential unsharability:

> [W]hen one speaks about "one's own physical pain" and about "another person's physical pain," one might almost appear to be speaking about two wholly distinct orders of events. For the person whose pain it is, it is "effortlessly" grasped (that is, even with the most heroic effort it cannot *not* be grasped); while for the person outside the sufferer's body, what is "effortless" is *not* grasping it (it is easy to remain wholly unaware of its existence; even with effort, one may remain in doubt about its existence or may retain the astonishing freedom of denying its existence; and, finally, if with the best effort of sustained attention one successfully apprehends it, the aversiveness of the "it" one apprehends will only be a shadowy fraction of the actual "it"). So, for the person in pain, so

---

42. For an ultimately unsuccessful attempt to assess the amount of pain caused by different methods of execution, see Harold Hillman, "The Possible Pain Experienced during Execution by Different Methods," *Perception* 22 (1993): 745–53. "It is difficult to know," Hillman writes, "how much pain the person being executed feels or for how long because many of the signs of pain are obscured by the procedure or by physical restraints." Hence, at best, "one can identify those steps which are likely to be painful" (745–55). This skeptical conclusion is not sufficient, however, to prevent Hillman from offering a chart in which he claims to identify the causes of pain occasioned by different methods of execution, the sort of sensation produced by each cause, and the intensity of each such sensation, although he does reluctantly confess that "the likely duration of the sensations is not known" (749).

incontestably and unnegotiably present is it that "having pain"
may come to be thought of as the most vibrant example of what it
is to "have certainty," while for the other person it is so elusive that
"hearing about pain" may exist as the primary model of what it is
"to have doubt."[43]

The radical solipsism of pain is, on Scarry's account, a function of the
fact that it, alone among interior states, has no referent beyond the body
itself (in contrast, say, to desire, which is always desire *for* something):
"Though the capacity to experience physical pain is as primal a fact
about the human being as is the capacity to hear, to touch, to desire, to
fear, to hunger, it differs from these events, and from every other bodily and psychic event, by not having an object in the external world."
As such, the experience of pain is to be sharply distinguished from that
of psychological suffering, which, "though often difficult for any one
person to express, *does* have referential content, *is* susceptible to verbal
objectification."[44] Acute physical pain, by way of contrast, encloses the
sufferer within a private universe made all the more desperate by the
realization that its agony points forever and only back upon itself.

Because pain is idiosyncratically nonreferential in this sense,
Scarry continues, it is singularly unresponsive to the claims of linguistic articulation: "This objectlessness, the complete absence of referential
content, almost prevents it from being rendered in language: objectless,
it cannot easily be objectified in any form, material or verbal." The
impoverishment of our contemporary vocabulary of pain is, therefore,
not a function of its modernist construction, nor of its interested appropriation by the profession of medicine, but of its ineluctable reality as
"a pure physical experience of negation, an immediate sensory rendering of 'against,' of something being against one, and of something one
must be against." Because that experience of aversiveness is indeed so
elemental, we should not be surprised to discover just how narrow is
the range of cultural variability with respect to ways of giving voice to
pain. Its limited scope "expose[s] and confirm[s] the universal sameness of the central problem, a problem that originates much less in the
inflexibility of any one language or in the shyness of any one culture
than in the utter rigidity of pain itself: its resistance to language is not

---

43. Elaine Scarry, *The Body in Pain: The Making and the Unmaking of the World* (New
York: Oxford University Press, 1985), 4.
44. Scarry, *The Body in Pain*, 161, 11.

simply one of its incidental or accidental attributes but is essential to what it is."[45]

Pain, Scarry continues, does not merely resist linguistic articulation; it also destroys the capacity to speak. Granted, when pain is unrelenting but not all-consuming, it may monopolize language, becoming its only subject, via the discourse of complaint. However, when acute and unyielding, it aggressively demolishes the contents of consciousness and, in so doing, eliminates our capacity to project ourselves into an intersubjective world of shared meanings: "At first occurring only as an appalling but limited internal fact, it eventually occupies the entire body and spills out into the realm beyond the body, takes over all that is inside and outside, makes the two obscenely indistinguishable, and systematically destroys anything like language or world extension that is alien to itself and threatening to its claims." As "the coherence of complaint is displaced by the sounds anterior to learned language,"[46] what was once a person becomes something ever less recognizable as a human being, ever more exclusively defined by its entrapment within a vicious circle of corporeal torment.

With this account, I believe, Scarry has offered an eloquent articulation of the distinguishing features of what I have called "modernist" pain. Her insistence on "the ironclad privacy of the body"[47] and so pain's essentially unsharable character, her representation of it as uniformly aversive, her Cartesian distinction between psychological suffering and physiological pain, and, finally, her conviction that language must remain forever frustrated in its efforts to represent this invisible interior reality, all betray her endorsement of a cluster of modernist presuppositions that would have been more or less unintelligible, for example, to Blaise Pascal. Scarry, of course, must reject this reading of her argument since it entails representing as culturally and historically specific what she must deem acontextual and timeless in order to sustain her affirmation of pain's "universal sameness" and, more particularly, her insistence upon its utter absence of referential content. Scarry's essentialism in this regard becomes problematic in a specifically political sense when it is joined to her contention that "the relative ease or difficulty with which any given phenomenon can be verbally represented also influences the ease or difficulty with which that phe-

45. Scarry, *The Body in Pain*, 162, 2, 5.
46. Scarry, *The Body in Pain*, 55, 54.
47. Scarry, *The Body in Pain*, 60.

nomenon comes to be politically represented."[48] If pain is indeed characterized by the sort of all-consuming brute facticity ascribed to it by
Scarry, then it is not clear how it can ever become a subject of political
representation, let alone contestation. That unhappy conclusion cannot
help but compromise the efforts of those, like Robert Cover, who seek
to highlight the mutual imbrication of law and pain, but who at the
same time are sufficiently taken with Scarry's argument to adopt it as
their own.[49]

Although I will only allude to it here, one way to call into question
Scarry's reading of the relationship between pain and language is to
affirm what she must deny, that is, the extensive cross-cultural variability apparent in discourses of pain.[50] The significance of that variability will be incompletely realized, however, so long as it remains
informed by the realist distinction, implicit in most discussions of
pain's cultural construction (and expressly affirmed by Ivan Illich
above), between the brute neurological reality of pain sensations and
culturally specific experiences of them.[51] So long as we endorse that
distinction, we will be tempted to embrace Scarry's contention that, in
speaking of pain, "the human voice must aspire to become a precise

---

48. Scarry, *The Body in Pain*, 12.

49. For his endorsement of Scarry's understanding of pain, see Cover, "Violence
and the Word," 1601–2.

50. For a helpful account of the distinguishing features of the English grammar of
pain, see Horacio Fabrega Jr. and Stephen Tyman, "Language and Cultural Influences in
the Description of Pain," *British Journal of Medical Psychology* 49 (1976): 349–71. For an
indication of the different ways several Asian languages fashion the experience of pain,
see Anthony Diller, "Cross-Cultural Pain Semantics," *Pain* 9 (1980): 9–26. Whereas the
English language of pain is defined, for the most part, by certain undifferentiated nouns
that are qualified adjectivally (e.g., "a sharp pain" or "a burning pain"), the Thai language is defined by a series of verbs that are less prone to such qualification because the
discriminations afforded by adjectives in English are already contained within them. It
should also be noted that the Thai discourse of pain draws no clear distinction between
what speakers of English label physiological as opposed to psychological or emotional
distress.

51. For an example of work that affirms the cultural variability of pain, but retains
the problematic distinction between its prediscursive reality and its linguistic formulation, see Horacio Fabrega Jr. and Stephen Tyma, "Culture, Language and the Shaping of
Illness: An Illustration Based on Pain," *Journal of Psychosomatic Research* 20 (1976): 323–37.
"To place the analysis in perspective, we have to remember that in rendering a description the individual has to first choose appropriate words which in his language label his
experience. Following this, he must place these words in more or less well formed utter-
ances which realize his grammatical rules. In the process, he renders pain as a linguistic
object" (325).

reflection of material reality,"[52] that is, to burrow beneath these various cultural articulations in order to discover the language that pain would itself speak, if only it could. Within a scientistic culture, that representationalist aspiration cannot help but bolster the medical profession's assertion of its own special competence to articulate the truth about pain, and the hegemonic pretense of that conviction, not the nature of pain itself, will make it exceedingly difficult to move toward a specifically political conception.

To enable such a conception, I propose that we begin by adopting a constructivist as opposed to a representationalist view of the relationship between language and pain. This is not to urge a simple discursivist reformulation of the behaviorist account of pain, that is, one that effectively equates the sentence "I am in pain" with the experience of being in pain or, still less plausibly, one that considers that sentence to be pain's cause. But it is to reject what Wittgenstein called the "picture" theory of language, one that in this instance regards *pain* as an inert label that merely describes or expresses an antecedent or extradiscursive object. To posit the reality of pain prior to or independent of language is still to posit that reality; and that very act of positing necessarily entails the invocation of a culturally specific and politically valenced construction of its alleged object. The work accomplished by that construction will go unrecognized so long as we forget, for example, that the figuration of pain as a mechanistic event caused by nociceptive impulses traveling along neural pathways between the site of tissue damage and the brain is less an indicator of pain's true nature than of the contemporary medical profession's success in defining that reality.

"We experience pain," contends David Morris, "only and entirely as we interpret it."[53] I take Morris to be claiming by this that all vocabularies of pain are quasi-performative in the sense that they participate in fashioning the reality they are said to represent; and this is so regardless of whether one considers the words we cite to communicate the intensity or qualitative dimensions of pain (e.g., *ache, searing, unbearable,* etc.) or the less nuanced but nonetheless meaningful sounds we make when pain more radically incapacitates (e.g., screaming, moaning, etc.). "[T]he manner in which pain is expressed—either in a reserved, contained fashion, or disclosed in an explosion of wails and

---

52. Scarry, *The Body in Pain,* 9.
53. Morris, *The Culture of Pain,* 29.

moans—has a direct relation to the way in which pain is actually borne and, in the fullest sense of the term, to what is actually felt. The very act of proclaiming one's pain, beyond what is actually manifested and beyond the meaning it projects, has a direct effect on the reality of the experience without our being able to fully determine whether the actual expression brings relief by liberating, or perhaps amplifies the feeling through an echoing phenomenon."[54] If Roselyne Rey is correct in this regard, then perhaps we should reconsider Scarry's contention that pain is defined by and distinguished from all other phenomena by its radical absence of any referential content. If the language of pain is constitutive of its object, then it seems more plausible to suggest that its intelligibility, indeed its recognizability *as* pain, is a function of whatever referential content it acquires via its discursive formulation. The absence of any designation for what we would call *pain* in the *Dictionnaire de théologie,* to recall an example cited earlier, should be sufficient to unsettle our received conviction that what the body endures can be segregated from the categories that render that suffering meaningful.

To note the cultural variability of pain's discourses is useful because it causes us to question the apparent self-evidence of the English grammar of pain, especially as it informs the biomechanical conception. To give this insight a constructivist twist is still better because we are thereby prompted to ask how language fashions the reality it is thought to mirror. Together, these moves cast doubt on Scarry's contention that the possibility of pain's political articulation is essentially compromised by the recalcitrant character of the object to be afforded voice. That difficulty, on my account, has more to do with our modernist construction of pain, which occludes its political dimensions, than with the nature of pain per se. That these dimensions are recoverable is indirectly intimated by the etymology of the term itself. The English word *pain* derives from a Latin noun *(poena)* that originally bore the sense of punishment, tax, penalty, or fine. Under the influence of Christianity, this term's associations with legal notions of wrongdoing and its rectification were partially displaced as it, although retaining the sense of punishment, came to refer more generically to an ineradicable mark of a sinful human condition. This, however, did not altogether eliminate the specifically legal sense of the term, a fact indicated by the presence in Old English of two terms *(pinian* and *peyne)* one of which suggested a notion of general suffering and the other pun-

54. Rey, *The History of Pain,* 4–5.

ishment for crime. Only after 1500 did these terms acquire sufficient phonological similarity to merge into the single term *pain*.[55] The gradual secularization of this abstract noun, especially via its medicalization in the nineteenth century, effectively extirpated all remaining associations with the concept of legal punishment.

Although no doubt too hasty, this etymological excursion hints at the possibility of recovering an expressly political account of pain. Ironically, Scarry herself realizes this possibility, if only in part, through her analysis of torture, which, she argues, involves the "transformation of body into voice"[56] or, more specifically, pain's translation into political power. The practice of torture subverts the categorical opposition between language and pain that Scarry must affirm for other purposes, and it does so in two ways. First, on her analysis, language can itself become a cause of pain, as it does during an interrogation: "The question, whatever its content, is an act of wounding; the answer, whatever its content, is a scream."[57] Second, and more important for my purposes, the body in pain can itself become something akin to a discursive artifact, one that speaks of and affirms the totality of sovereign power:

> While torture contains language, specific human words and sounds, it is itself a language, an objectification, an acting out. Real pain, agonizing pain, is inflicted on a person; but torture, which contains specific acts of inflicting pain, is also itself a demonstration and magnification of the felt-experience of pain. In the very processes it uses to produce pain within the body of the prisoner, it bestows visibility on the structure and enormity of what is usually private and incommunicable, contained within the boundaries of the sufferer's body. It then goes on to deny, to falsify, the reality of the very thing it has itself objectified by a perceptual shift which converts the vision of suffering into the wholly illusory but, to the torturers and the regime they represent, wholly convincing spectacle of power. The physical pain is so incontestably real that it seems to confer its quality of "incontestable reality" on that power that has brought it into being.[58]

---

55. See Fabrega and Tyman, "Language and Cultural Influences," for a helpful chart that tracks the etymological shifts I have recapitulated in abbreviated form here.

56. Scarry, *The Body in Pain*, 45.

57. Scarry, *The Body in Pain*, 46.

58. Scarry, *The Body in Pain*, 27.

In acknowledging torture's status as a language, Scarry effectively concedes that the pain occasioned by that meaningful practice is itself discursively mediated. Were that not the case, were pain as "monolithically consistent in its assault on language"[59] as she suggests elsewhere, then it would be unavailable for political appropriation in the interest of buttressing claims to incontestable power.

What I wish to ask in closing is whether there is any reason to believe, as Scarry apparently does, that pain can *only* be politically appropriated in the service of affirming state power. If, as she insists, recourse to torture is itself a sign of regime instability, is it possible that the pain implicated in the law's very existence might be rendered visible in a way that discloses the contestability of state power? That this possibility is unimaginable to Scarry is made clear when she contends that, if we are to prevent pain from being converted into a regime's fiction of power, without exception we must insist that it be referred back to the suffering human body: "The failure to express pain—whether the failure to objectify its attributes or instead the failure, once those attributes are objectified, to refer them to their original site in the human body—will *always* work to allow its appropriation and conflation with debased forms of power; conversely, the successful expression of pain will *always* work to expose and make impossible that appropriation and conflation."[60] No matter how ethically commendable, what this claim fails to recognize is that so long as the pain referred back to the human body is construed in modernist biomedical terms, as state agents are all too quick to do, it will be rendered solipsistic, deniable, and immune to political engagement.

Scarry argues that "at particular moments when there is within a society a crisis of belief—that is, when some central idea or ideology or cultural construct has ceased to elicit a population's belief either because it is manifestly fictitious or because it has for some reason been divested of ordinary forms of substantiation—the sheer material factualness of the human body will be borrowed to lend that cultural construct the aura of 'realness' and 'certainty.'"[61] Is it possible that our understanding of the normative status of pain within the law is itself a cultural construct that has now been "divested of ordinary forms of substantiation" and so become questionable? Is that not precisely what

---

59. Scarry, *The Body in Pain*, 13.
60. Scarry, *The Body in Pain*, 14; emphasis added.
61. Scarry, *The Body in Pain*, 14.

we would expect within a late liberal state that can no longer provide persuasive justification for the harm it inflicts upon those whose bodies, in the last analysis, are incidental to their status as juridical persons? Is it possible that the palpable body in pain, once an indispensable means of substantiating the state's claim to authority, now threatens to delegitimate that same claim? Is not the horror elicited by the blood shed by Allen Lee Davis an indication of just such a crisis? And if that is so, then how might Davis's blood become the sort of discursive artifact that raises questions not about whether he did or did not experience pain, but about just how completely a liberal regime can obscure the violence that is essential to its initial foundation as well as it ongoing integrity as a state?

As I noted in this essay's introduction, the troublesome implications of the violence that is integral to the late liberal body politic are checked, in large measure, by demarcating and then policing sharp boundaries between the legislative institutions that adopt capital punishment statutes, the judicial organs that impose death sentences, and the executive officials that make live bodies dead; and, as I have tried to show over the course of the preceding pages, the security of these boundaries is reinforced by a biomedical conception of pain that locates suffering squarely within the opaque confines of the body's interior. If these insidiously complementary border projects are to be politicized, perhaps we ought not to insist on "the sheer material factualness of the human body." Perhaps, instead, we should affirm what Scarry elsewhere calls the body's "referential instability."[62] To do so is not to argue that the body can be free of all referential content. Rather, it is to ask under what conditions the rationalized body of late modernity might be stripped of its apparent self-evidence as well as how that body's pain, extricated from the confines of a medicalized construction, might begin to overflow these boundaries and so, like the blood spilling from Allen Lee Davis, to wash throughout the regime that now struggles so assiduously to contain it.

In one sense, this is to ask whether, under the conditions of late modernity, it is possible to articulate something akin to the sort of theologically inspired narrative that, in order to restore the integrity of an injured body politic, required that Damiens's pain be disseminated throughout the realm. Yet, in another sense, this project must be quite

---

62. Scarry, *The Body in Pain*, 121.

different. If the politicization of pain is to contribute to specifically democratic ends, we must reject any effort to fashion a single narrative of the body in order to counter that proffered by biomedicine and all too eagerly endorsed by the law. Only a proliferation of diverse narratives of embodiment, no one of which is deemed incontestably true, can begin to unsettle the antipolitical alliance of a medical profession that affirms its hegemonic authority over the meaning of pain and a state that affirms its monopolistic control over the means of legitimate violence.

The Sacred Name of Pain: The Role of Victim Impact Evidence in Death Penalty Sentencing Decisions

Jennifer L. Culbert

Victim impact evidence is information about the financial, emotional, and physical effects of a criminal act on a victim or the members of a victim's family.[1] In 1990, in *Payne v. Tennessee*, the Supreme Court held that the Eighth Amendment does not prohibit a state from permitting victim impact evidence to be heard by a jury making a sentencing decision in a capital trial.[2] The Court's decision to allow such evidence to be presented to a jury during the sentencing phase of a capital trial continues to be controversial, due in part to the fact that in 1988 in *South Carolina v. Gathers*, and two years before that in *Booth v. Maryland* (1986), the Court had found that hearing victim impact evidence in capital cases violated the Eighth Amendment's prohibition against cruel and

I would like to thank Madelaine Adelman, Marianne Constable, Peter Fitzpatrick, Lisa Garbus, Jeffrie Murphy, Austin Sarat, Karl Shoemaker, Helen Thompson, David Wittenberg, and two anonymous reviewers for their comments.

1. Philip Talbert identifies four basic types of victim impact evidence: (1) the victim's statements about the crime, including descriptions of the physical harm they suffered and the lasting effects of the crime; (2) statements made by relatives or close friends about the victim's personality, relationships with others, and general contributions to the community; (3) statements made by members of the family regarding the emotional impact of the crime on themselves; and (4) statements made by relatives and close friends about their opinions of the crime, the defendant, and what the defendant deserves as punishment for having committed such a crime. "The Relevance of Victim Impact Statements to the Criminal Sentencing Decision," *U.C.L.A. Law Review* 36 (1988): 199–232.

2. *Payne v. Tennessee*, 501 U.S. 808, 827 (1990).

unusual punishment.[3] In this essay I examine the subtle but significant effect of the Supreme Court's decision about victim impact evidence in death penalty cases. Specifically, I observe that victim impact evidence in capital trials provides judges with a unique moral power in a liberal, pluralist society. Such a society is committed to the idea that individuals conduct their lives according to values and ends they identify and choose for themselves. Thus, individuals may choose to subscribe to one of a variety of what John Rawls calls "comprehensive doctrines," or conceptions of justice that cover all recognized values and virtues within a precisely articulated system.[4]

However, in such a society, those who would judge others—either as members of society, members of a jury, or members of the bench—are more or less condemned to the sincere but ethically banal and morally unsatisfactory position that "everything is relative." Victim impact evidence liberates the sentencing authority in death penalty cases (at least) from this state of suspended moral animation. Because of the universal and yet unique character of the experience to which the families of murder victims testify, victim impact statements may ground and legitimate judgments made in, by, and on behalf of the members of a pluralist state. The pain and suffering expressed by the murder victim's survivors can serve as an absolute in a society in which every other kind of claim is subject to contestation, doubt, and criticism.[5] In brief, after the Supreme Court's ruling in *Payne v. Tennessee*, those who must pass judgment in death penalty cases may now turn to expressions of pain as others may once have turned to God, in trust that

---

3. *Booth v. Maryland*, 482 U.S. 496 (1986); *South Carolina v. Gathers*, 490 U.S. 805 (1988). In *Furman v. Georgia*, 408 U.S. 238 (1972), the Supreme Court says that any factor that renders "arbitrary" the decision to sentence a criminal to death makes capital punishment cruel and unusual, and hence unconstitutional. In *Booth*, and again in *Gathers*, the Court finds that victim impact evidence primarily appeals to the emotions of the sentencing authority, thereby making it difficult for the sentencing authority to make a rational or "nonarbitrary" sentencing decision. Consequently, the Court finds that the admission of victim impact evidence violates the Eighth Amendment. For the details of *Booth v. Maryland* and *South Carolina v. Gathers* see below.

4. The term "comprehensive doctrine" is discussed by John Rawls, *Political Liberalism* (New York: Columbia University Press, 1996), 13.

5. The parallel between victims of the Holocaust and victims of the murders that occur everyday in the United States is reinforced by the tendency of some victims' rights advocates to refer to the people who lose loved ones in random acts of violence as "survivors." See *Payne v. Tennessee*, 835–44.

this "sacred name" will make it possible for individuals to answer the question, "In the name of what or whom do we judge?"[6]

The first section of this essay examines the Court's decision in *Payne v. Tennessee* against the backdrop of its earlier decisions in *Booth v. Maryland* and *South Carolina v. Gathers,* and considers several explanations for the sudden change in the Court's position on the admissibility of victim impact evidence in death penalty cases. In the next section of the essay, the Court's ruling is reconsidered in terms of the philosophical context in which it takes place. The third section demonstrates how these terms are helpful in describing the relevance of victim impact evidence to sentencing decisions in death penalty cases. Drawing from the work of Friedrich Nietzsche, the essay concludes with some critical reflections on what the Court's attitude toward victim impact evidence says about contemporary American society and what its attitudes bode for the future of our capital punishment jurisprudence.

Legal Backdrop

In 1986, in *Booth v. Maryland,* the Supreme Court considered for the first time whether the Eighth Amendment prohibits a capital sentencing jury from considering victim impact evidence. The petitioner, John Booth, was found guilty of robbing and brutally murdering Irvine Bronstein, seventy-eight, and his wife Rose, seventy-five. For these crimes, Booth was sentenced to death. He appealed his sentence on the grounds that a victim impact statement prepared by the state and submitted to the jury during the sentencing phase of his trial injected an "arbitrary factor" into the jury's sentencing decision.[7] The statement was based on interviews with the Bronsteins' son, daughter, son-in-

---

6. This particular formulation of the problem of judgment in a pluralist society is drawn from Philippe Lacoue-Labarthe, *Heidegger, Art, and Politics: The Fiction of the Political,* trans. Chris Turner (Oxford: Basil Blackwell, 1990), 31.

7. In 1986, at least thirty-nine states permitted or required victim impact statements at sentencing. See the United States Department of Justice report *Five Years Later: A Report on the President's Task Force on Victims of Crime* (Washington, D.C.: U.S. Government Printing Office, 1986), 4. According to the *1996 Victims' Rights Source Book* (Washington, D.C.: National Victim Center, 2000) presently every state allows victim impact evidence at sentencing—either through input into the presentence report or through presentation of a written or oral statement at the sentencing hearing (221).

law, and granddaughter, who testified to the victims' outstanding personal qualities and how deeply they would be missed. In addition, relatives spoke about the emotional and personal problems the family faced as a result of the murders. The Supreme Court agreed with Booth that this evidence was prejudicial. The Court stated that when a jury is deciding upon sentence during the penalty phase of a capital trial, it may consider only two issues: the defendant's background and record, and the circumstances of the crime. The Court found that information about the impact of the crime on the victim's family and information about their views on the defendant and his or her crime shed little light on these areas of concern. Indeed, the Court said that information provided in victim impact statements serves only to inflame the jury and to divert it from its sole duty: to determine the defendant's culpability in the commission of the crime for which he or she was convicted.

In *South Carolina v. Gathers* (1988), the Supreme Court reiterated that defendants' punishments must reflect their personal responsibility and moral guilt. In this case, Demetrius Gathers was convicted of murder and sentenced to death for the killing of Richard Haynes. While the state presented no victim impact evidence during the sentencing phase of the trial, in his closing argument the prosecutor commented extensively on the victim's character and suggested that Gathers deserved the death penalty because Haynes had been a religious man and a good citizen. The Court affirmed the decision of the Supreme Court of South Carolina to remand the case for a new sentencing proceeding. As the defendant did not know the victim was a devout Christian and a registered voter when he killed him, the Court said that such details were irrelevant to the jury's deliberations about the defendant's blameworthiness. That is, the Court found that information the defendant did not know about the victim could not be admitted for the jury's consideration at sentencing because it had no bearing on the crime the defendant committed.

However, two years later in *Payne v. Tennessee* (1990), the Court indicated that it had ruled incorrectly in both *Booth* and *Gathers*. In this case, Pervis Tyrone Payne was convicted of murdering Charisse Christopher and her two-year-old daughter, Lacie, with a butcher knife. He was also found guilty of assault with intent to commit first-degree murder for attacking Christopher's three-year-old son, Nicholas. During the sentencing phase of Payne's trial, Christopher's mother, Nicholas's grandmother, testified about the psychological effects of the murders on the boy, and in his closing argument the prosecutor revisited Nicholas's lonely suffering from the moment when Payne left him for dead on the kitchen floor. The jury sentenced Payne to death for the two murders and to thirty years in prison for the assault on Nicholas. Payne appealed his sentences on the grounds that the grandmother's testimony and the state's closing arguments should not have been admitted. However, when the case reached the Supreme Court, the Court refused to honor its own earlier decisions on the matter. Instead, the Court reversed itself and found that the Eighth Amendment does not necessarily prohibit a capital sentencing jury from considering victim impact evidence.

In *Payne*, the Court offers several reasons for its decision to violate the principle of *stare decisis*, the policy of courts to stand by precedent and not to disturb settled points of law. First, the Court argues that victim impact evidence provides more complete descriptions of the crime for which the defendant is being sentenced. While the point of the penalty phase of a capital trial is to determine what punishment fits the defendant's crime, the Court says that an appropriate punishment may not be found if the magnitude of the crime is not fully appreciated. Second, the Court claims that the scales of justice are weighted unfairly in favor of the defendant in a capital trial. According to the Court, during the penalty phase of a capital trial the defendant may present the jury with almost any aspect of his or her personal circumstances or background as a reason for a sentence less than death. By contrast, the state may draw only from a limited number of aggravating circumstances set out by law to argue for the appropriateness of the death penalty. To rectify the imbalance caused by this discrepancy, the Court says, the state should be able to tell a jury about the life the defendant took and the ramifications of that act for the victim's family and society at large. Third, the Court notes that its interpretation of the Eighth Amendment does not preclude the jury from hearing about the uniqueness of the defendant's victim. Finally, the Court asserts that such information will help the trial court redress some of the harm caused by the defendant. As Justice Sandra Day O'Connor observes in her concurring opinion:

> [Murder] transforms a living person with hopes, dreams and fears into a corpse, thereby taking away all that is special and unique about the person. The Constitution does not preclude a State from deciding to give some of that back. (832)

While the reasons the Court offers in support of its ruling in *Payne v. Tennessee* are compelling, they are not particularly new. In his *Booth* dissent, for example, Justice Byron White argues that the full extent of the harm caused by a convicted murderer includes the harm to the victim's family (516). In her *Gathers* dissent, O'Connor argues that the judgment required of a capital sentencer is one-sided because defendants are permitted to present a wide range of information about their background while the prosecution is prohibited from so much as giving the sentencer a "glimpse of the life" they took (816–17). Why in *Payne* does the Court now find these reasons so forceful as to warrant reversing its previous decisions?

The most obvious explanation is offered by Justice Thurgood Marshall. In his *Payne* dissent, Marshall puts it bluntly: "Neither the law nor the facts supporting *Booth* and *Gathers* underwent any change in the last four years. Only the personnel of this Court did" (844).[8] As there is nothing new in the majority's discussion of the problems with *Booth* and *Gathers,* Marshall concludes that the Court bases its decision to overrule these precedents not on reason but on "the proclivities of the individuals who now comprise a majority of this Court" (851). Marshall recognizes that there are circumstances under which the Court may depart from precedent—that "the doctrine of *stare decisis* is not an 'inexorable command'" (849)—however, he argues that none of these circumstances apply to *Booth* or *Gathers* (849).[9] In short, he claims that the majority is ideologically rather than rationally inspired to change the constitutional order. What is more, he accuses the majority of using its power to ignore the doctrine of *stare decisis,* no matter what the consequences for the rule of law.

The tone of moral outrage Marshall assumes in his dissent may sound a bit naive (or disingenuous) to students of the Supreme Court. Changes in the tenor of the Court's decisions are to be expected with

---

8. In 1988, Justice Anthony Kennedy replaced Justice Lewis Powell, and in 1990, Justice David Souter replaced Justice William Brennan.

9. Marshall recognizes three "special justifications" for overruling a precedent: (1) the advent of "subsequent changes or developments in the law" that undermine a decision's rationale; (2) the need "to bring [a decision] into agreement with experience and with facts newly ascertained"; and (3) a showing that a particular precedent has become a "detriment to coherence and consistency in the law" (849). The majority claims that *Booth* and *Gathers* "have defied consistent application by the lower courts," but Marshall finds the evidence it offers in support of this claim to be so feeble as to be ridiculous (850).

changes in the Court's personnel. After all, Supreme Court justices are nominated by the president and confirmed by the Senate.[10] When nominating persons to the Supreme Court, the president looks for individuals who are qualified for the position. However, he also looks for individuals who share his view of the world. True, justices are constrained from arbitrarily deciding cases by the conventions of judicial decision making—in particular, the use of legal reasoning and the adherence to precedent. Yet these conventions do not prevent justices from reaching "creative" or "innovative" decisions.[11] In a recent book on the Supreme Court, James Simon documents how William Rehnquist has, since becoming chief justice in 1986, encouraged the Court to make just such decisions.[12] In particular, Simon notes how Rehnquist takes advantage of his right as chief justice to assign himself the task of drafting the Court's opinions when he is in the majority and how, in this position, Rehnquist may analyze the questions put before the Court in such a way as to reopen settled questions of constitutional law.[13]

---

10. Since 1789, 107 persons have taken the oath of office as members of the United States Supreme Court, and the Senate has rejected only twelve nominees. For more details about Supreme Court nominees and their fates, see Harold J. Spaeth and Edward Conrad Smith, eds., *The Constitution of the United States*, 13th ed. (New York: Harper-Collins, 1991).

11. In his analysis of the Supreme Court's ability to influence public policy, Harold J. Spaeth argues that Americans cherish the idea that judicial decisions are objective. Consequently, he says, they refuse to recognize judges as policymakers. According to Spaeth, this refusal reflects a childish desire to be able to turn to someone for protection from the contingencies of the real (adult) world and to be told what to do by a power beyond reproach. See *Supreme Court Policy Making: Explanation and Prediction* (San Francisco: W. H. Freeman, 1979), 8.

12. James F. Simon, *The Center Holds: The Power Struggle inside the Rehnquist Court* (New York: Simon and Schuster, 1995). Simon's analysis of the Rehnquist Court is noted here not to criticize the chief justice but rather to make an observation about common Court practice.

13. *Payne v. Tennessee* provides a good example of Rehnquist's judicial activism. Writing for the majority in *Payne*, Rehnquist observes: "Considerations in favor of *stare decisis* are at their acme in cases involving property and contract rights, where reliance interests are involved[;] the opposite is true in cases such as the present one involving procedural and evidentiary rules" (828; citations omitted). While the question before the Court concerns victim impact evidence, Rehnquist takes this opportunity to state that the doctrine of *stare decisis* applies primarily to the conditions that make commercial activity possible: property and contract rights. With this statement, Rehnquist invites lower courts to challenge any of the Supreme Court's existing civil rights decisions and implies that in the future the Court will not necessarily employ the same principles it used in the past in deciding cases concerning procedural and evidentiary rules.

Of course, the Court itself states that it overrules *Booth* and *Gathers* because these decisions are unworkable and badly reasoned (827). Writing for the majority, Rehnquist observes that lower courts have been unable to apply the decisions in a consistent fashion. He also notes that the Court's decisions in both *Booth* and *Gathers* were strongly contested and were decided finally by only the narrowest of margins. Although he says adhering to precedent is usually "the wise policy," Rehnquist argues that the Court is not constrained to do so, especially when a case involves a constitutional question. He says that in such cases the Supreme Court alone is in a position to review the record critically and correct any past mistakes. Indeed, he writes, it has a duty to do so.

As the highest court in the country, the Supreme Court is the only judicial institution in the United States in a position to overrule a previous Supreme Court decision. While the individuals who serve on the Court are not infallible, the Court has final word on the principles involved in the proper adjudication of any legal dispute so that such disputes may be settled once and for all. However, while the Court alone is empowered to decide when it has decided an issue "incorrectly," or when the circumstances have changed so that the Court's earlier ruling is no longer appropriate, it must be careful not to reverse itself often. As Marshall notes in his *Payne* dissent, lower courts rely on the Court to respect and defend the principle of the rule of law. Should the Court reverse itself frequently and capriciously, deciding cases would become, in effect, the "mere exercise of judicial will with arbitrary and unpredictable results" (cited 849). The entire legal system would lose its capacity to resolve legal disputes with any authority. Consequently, the Court reverses precedent only under special circumstances.[14] Given this understanding of the significance of the doctrine of *stare decisis*, a critical examination of the circumstances Rehnquist cites to justify the reversal of precedent in *Payne* is warranted. Upon examination, the circumstances that Rehnquist cites—in particular, the fact that *Booth* and *Gathers* were decided by narrow majorities and that the dissent in both cases was "spirited"—do not seem particularly

---

14. However, in an article about the implications of the Court's ruling in *Teague v. Lane* (1989), Linda Meyer argues that over the last ten years or so the Supreme Court has gradually undermined the power of precedent and put judges in the position of deciding cases by fiat. See "'Nothing We Say Matters': *Teague* and New Rules," *University of Chicago Law Review* 61 (1994): 423–92.

remarkable. Indeed, many precedent-establishing cases may be similarly described.

Such observations lend credence to a third explanation of the Court's decision to change its position on the admissibility of victim impact evidence in capital cases. Commentators suggest that the Court changes its position in response to pressure from the public. That the Supreme Court responds to the "sense of justice of the people" is broadly recognized, and in *Furman v. Georgia* (1972), Marshall himself argues that public opinion is an appropriate reason for ignoring the doctrine of *stare decisis*. In *Furman*, he claims that capital punishment violates the Eighth Amendment not because it is "objectively" excessive punishment, but because it is "morally unacceptable" to the people of the United States (360).

A growing victims' rights movement is based on the idea that the criminal justice system has generally ignored the needs and interests of victims of crime and should become more responsive to these concerns. According to Marlene Young, the executive director of the National Organization for Victim Assistance (NOVA), the movement developed from efforts in the 1960s and 1970s to establish witness/victim programs, to pass victim compensation legislation, and to assist victims of domestic violence and rape.[15] The variety of victim assistance programs in the United States reflects the diverse origins of the victims' rights movement. In addition to NOVA, among the most well known programs are the National Victim Center, Mothers Against Drunk Driving (MADD), Society's League Against Molesters (SLAM), the Victims' Assistance Legal Organization (VALOR), and Parents of Murdered Children. In addition to establishing a variety of support and advocacy groups, the victims' rights movement has successfully lobbied for both state and federal legislation.[16] It has also been working to pass an amendment to the Constitution of the United States. The most

---

15. Marlene A. Young, "Emerging Issues in Victim Assistance," *Pepperdine Law Review* 17 (1989): 129–43.

16. According to the National Victims' Constitutional Amendment Network (NVCAN), as of May 2000, thirty-one states had amended their state constitutions to insure rights for crime victims. Frank Carrington, the executive director of VALOR, and Judge George Nicholson observe that state legislatures have been particularly quick to respond to the concerns voiced by the victims' rights movement. They also note that all branches of the federal government have recently recognized that crime victims have legal rights and have acted to protect those rights. See "Victims' Rights: An Idea Whose Time Has Come—Five Years Later: The Maturing of an Idea," *Pepperdine Law Review* 17 (1989): 1–18.

recent version of a Victims' Bill of Rights Constitutional Amendment was introduced for consideration during the 106th Congress in January 1999.[17]

Critics of the victims' rights movement suggest that the decision to permit victim impact evidence during the sentencing phase of capital trials is the product of an ideological struggle fought by wealthy, vocal victims predisposed to seek revenge or retaliation for harms suffered.[18] However, by blaming a small group of rich, wounded people for the Court's decision to change the law of the United States, we fail to attend to the significant consequences of the Court's change of heart. Specifically, we fail to appreciate how the Court's decision affects the discourse with which capital punishment is legitimated in a pluralist society. In such a society, judges and jurors are permitted to make an irrevocable decision about what a particular defendant deserves as punishment for a particular crime. Yet despite efforts to rationalize capital sentencing procedures, this decision remains an arbitrary one. The Court's decision to permit victim impact statements in capital trials

---

17. After an amendment by Senator Hatch in October 1999, the proposed amendment reads in part:

Section 1. A victim of a crime of violence, as these terms may be defined by law, shall have the rights:

—to reasonable notice of, and not to be excluded from, any public proceedings relating to the crime;

—to be heard, if present, and to submit a statement at all such proceedings to determine a conditional release from custody, an acceptance of a negotiated plea, or a sentence;

—to the foregoing rights at a parole proceeding that is not public, to the extent those rights are afforded to the convicted offender;

—to reasonable notice of and an opportunity to submit a statement concerning any proposed pardon or commutation of a sentence;

—to reasonable notice of a release or escape from custody relating to the crime;

—to consideration of the interest of the victim that any trial be free from unreasonable delay;

—to an order of restitution from the convicted offender;

—to consideration for the safety of the victim in determining any conditional release from custody relating to the crime; and

—to reasonable notice of the rights established by this article.

For the full text of the proposed amendment see <http://www.nvcan.org/docs/sjr3rs.htm>.

18. My thanks to an anonymous reviewer of this essay for reminding me of this point.

marks a (not necessarily conscious) shift in the discourse with which fatal and final decisions may be legitimated in a society in which individuals do not necessarily share the same assumptions or appeal to the same principles to guide or ground their judgments.[19]

In this essay, I offer another possible explanation of the Court's decision to change its interpretation of the Eighth Amendment. This explanation takes a wider view of the Court's ruling in *Payne v. Tennessee*. In brief, I suggest that the Court's ruling in favor of admitting victim impact evidence in death penalty cases embraces new means of legitimating moral decisions. The Court need not have acted with the intent to realize this potential of victim impact evidence, but our understanding of the Court's decision in *Payne v. Tennessee* would be limited if we failed to take into account the broader effects of its actions. The stories of loss, pain, and suffering that may now be heard during the penalty phase of capital trials provide judges and jurors with the kind of evidence the capital punishment system needs to be able to justify the finality of a sentence of death in a pluralist society. The rest of this essay will flesh out this explanation of the Court's ruling in *Payne v. Tennessee*.

Philosophical Context

As I have suggested, judges and jurors in our society appear condemned to the sincere but ethically banal and morally unsatisfactory position that "everything is relative." The philosophy of moral relativism asserts that there are no objective universal criteria of moral truth. Judgments vary between different cultures, different generations, and even different individuals, but no set of judgments has any more claim to truth than any other. Phillipa Foot argues that any judgment of "right" or "wrong" implicitly invokes the standards set by a

---

19. To remind ourselves of what is at stake here, consider the cynicism with which the verdict in the O. J. Simpson trial was met. Both the wealth of the defendant and the racial composition of the jury continue to be understood to have affected the outcome of the trial. Consider also a controversial article published in the *New Yorker* that argues that the dramatic increase in the number of hung juries over the past two decades is due to "black women contrarians," that is to say, African-American women jurors who are skeptical about the police, have strong religious convictions, and do not want to send more young black men to jail. See Jeffrey Rosen, "One Angry Woman," *New Yorker*, February 24–March 3, 1997, 54–64.

particular paradigm.[20] Outside of that particular paradigm, these judgments no longer make sense. Thus, where a basic ethical value of one society or individual conflicts with that of another, ethical relativism insists that no principled way of judging between them exists.

Over the past twenty-odd years, ever since the Supreme Court ruled in *Gregg v. Georgia* (1976) that capital punishment is constitutional, the Court has been constantly challenged to justify, clarify, and defend the grounds upon which the decision to sentence a person to death may be made.[21] The Court's inability to provide definitive answers to the questions raised by its commitment to the twin objectives of the capital punishment system, individual consideration and equal treatment,[22] has led to what Robert Weisberg calls the "deregulation of death." Weisberg argues that after a period of trying to rationalize the imposition of the death penalty in this country, the Court has effectively thrown up its hands and given up the task of containing capital punishment within the rule of law.[23] According to Weisberg, the Supreme Court has decided that it no longer can use constitutional law to foster legal formulas for regulating moral choice (395). By default, it decides to leave the decision to kill to the discretion of the sentencing authority. In so doing, the Court effectively returns to the position expressed by Justice Harlan in *McGautha v. California* (1971), that in a society of plural values, "Conflict of value is not a pathology of culture, but a natural aspect of the very phenomenon of having values" (394).

The distribution of death sentences in the United States provides strong evidence of the conflict of values in the United States. As Franklin Zimring and Gordon Hawkins observe, more executions have taken place in the South than in all other regions of the United States combined.[24] Texas continues to lead the country in the number of people put to death each year.[25] Zimring and Hawkins speculate that a history of frequent executions serves as a kind of precedent that reassures

---

20. Phillipa Foot, "Moral Relativism," in *Relativism: Cognitive and Moral*, ed. Jack W. Meiland and Michael Krausz (Notre Dame: University of Notre Dame Press, 1982), 160.

21. *Gregg v. Georgia*, 428 U.S. 153 (1976).

22. See *Eddings v. Oklahoma*, 455 U.S. 105 (1982).

23. Robert Weisberg, "Deregulating Death," *Supreme Court Review* 8 (1983): 305–95.

24. Franklin E. Zimring and Gordon Hawkins, *Capital Punishment and the American Agenda* (Cambridge: Cambridge University Press, 1986), 30.

25. According to figures supplied by the Death Penalty Information Center, thirty-five people were executed in Texas in 1999. Virginia, the state with the second largest number, executed fourteen people.

reluctant politicians, judges, and jurors that their own participation in executions is neither inhumane nor immoral (144). The Supreme Court refuses to intervene and review the laws that may give rise to this pattern. As Justice Anthony Kennedy observes in *McCleskey v. Zant* (1991), "Our federal system recognizes the independent power of a State to articulate societal norms through criminal law. But the power of a State to pass laws means little if the State cannot enforce them."[26]

However, once we have recognized a plurality of values in the context of a judgment that is, in a secular society, an absolute judgment, we inevitably return to the questions raised by Albert Camus in his discussion of capital punishment. In his famous essay "Reflections on the Guillotine," Camus claims that "Capital judgment upsets the only indisputable human solidarity—our solidarity against death—and it can be legitimized only by a truth or a principle that is superior to man."[27] If we have learned nothing else from the experience of World War II, Camus says, we have learned that humans are not naturally good, only worse or better. And as no one can lay claim to absolute innocence, no one can pose as a supreme judge and pronounce the supreme sentence. As human beings we can know enough to say that this or that major criminal deserves hard labor for life, but we cannot know enough to decree that he or she may not have a future (230).

The Supreme Court's decision to permit victim impact evidence to be heard during the sentencing phase of a capital trial may be explained as a response to this kind of "nihilistic" view, a view one critic characterizes as "denying the very possibility of a moral community in our time."[28] If this is the case, it is not surprising that the Court would permit survivors of murder victims to express their pain and suffering during the penalty phase of capital trials, for the feelings they manifest authorize the members of a diverse community to make final judgments.

I acknowledge that I am making a somewhat counterintuitive claim, particularly as critics of victim impact statements argue that victim impact statements permit, if not indulge, the play of prejudice in sentencing decisions. As prosecutors are already well aware, the more

---

26. *McCleskey v. Zant*, 494 U.S. 467, 473 (1991).

27. Albert Camus, "Reflections on the Guillotine (1957)," in *Resistance, Rebellion, and Death*, trans. Justin O'Brien (New York: Vintage International, 1988), 222.

28. Walter Berns, *For Capital Punishment: Crime and the Morality of the Death Penalty* (Lanham, Md.: University Press of America, 1979), 156.

attractive and sympathetic the victim is, the more heinous the crime appears, and the more deserving of punishment the criminal becomes.[29] The same effect is generated when survivors present themselves to testify to their pain and suffering. Indeed, critics have claimed that the comfort and eloquence of those willing to testify to their pain and suffering in the wake of the murder of a family member will unfairly affect sentencing decisions. To make matters worse, the poise and confidence with which individuals speak will often be a function of their cultural and class backgrounds. Thus, when judges and jurors are permitted to hear victim impact statements various forms of prejudice will be given more room for play in the sentencing of defendants in capital trials. All of these criticisms suggest that victim impact statements only make more evident the partial nature of justice in death penalty cases.

I personally find no reason to disagree with these observations. Yet how do critics of victim impact statements explain the Court's attitude? Surely the Court is aware that the capital punishment system already appears arbitrary in its privileging of some victims over others. I suggest that the inclusion of victim impact evidence may be perceived as a remedy for this very ill insofar as the pain and suffering presented in victim impact statements affirms rather than denies the grounds of our shared humanity. As many commentators have noted, evidence presented in the Baldus study suggesting that the murderers of whites are punished more severely than the murderers of blacks does not necessarily support an argument in favor of abolishing capital punishment.[30] In fact, this evidence may be used to support an argument in favor of executing more defendants, specifically more defendants who have been convicted of killing African-Americans. In other words, rather than interpreting evidence of bias in the capital punishment system as

29. Mark Costanzo, *Just Revenge: Costs and Consequences of the Death Penalty* (New York: St. Martin's Press, 1997), 83.

30. The Baldus study is a sophisticated statistical analysis that famously showed that defendants found guilty of killing white victims are always more likely than any other defendants to be sentenced to death. In *McCleskey v. Kemp*, the Supreme Court considered and responded to the Baldus study. In its holding, the Court was willing to accept the study's legitimacy but refused to overturn the petitioner's death sentence on the grounds that he had failed to prove that he personally had been discriminated against by the trial court or the State of Georgia. In addition, the Court observed that if it acted on the Baldus study, the entire criminal justice system would be put in jeopardy by evidence of racial discrimination in sentencing. In his dissent, Justice Blackmun accused the majority of being afraid of "too much justice." See *McCleskey v. Kemp*, 481 U.S. 279 (1987).

a reason for condemning it, one might understand this evidence as a reason for permitting more people to share their suffering with judges and jurors in order to overcome bias based on ignorance and a false sense of "us" versus "them."

Critics of victim impact statements inadvertently lend support to the claim that victim impact statements provide or reveal grounds for "absolute" or final decisions in a pluralist society. They do so most clearly when they express concern about the emotional impact this testimony will have on unwitting judges and jurors. For example, in an article deploring the Court's decision in *Payne v. Tennessee,* Catherine Bendor argues, "The only clear role for this evidence is to serve as a direct appeal to the emotional sympathies of the jurors."[31] Evidence intended to appeal to the emotional sympathies of jurors is not supposed to be considered admissible in death penalty cases. Since *Gregg v. Georgia,* as Justice John Stevens observes in his *Payne* dissent, "[The Supreme Court's] capital punishment jurisprudence requires any decision to impose the death penalty to be based on reason rather than caprice or emotion" (858). However, Bendor's argument against the Court's decision in *Payne* does not only point out a possible contradiction in the Court's capital punishment jurisprudence; it also reveals the ubiquity of the assumption that the sentencing authority in capital cases will find it difficult, if not impossible, to resist identifying with the survivors' suffering.[32] In her critique of the Court's decision, Bendor takes for granted that stories of pain and suffering will appeal to the unthinking part of the sentencing authority and will influence the

---

31. Catherine Bendor, "Defendants' Wrongs and Victims' Rights: *Payne v. Tennessee,* 111 S.Ct. 2597 (1991)," *Harvard Civil Rights–Civil Liberties Law Review* 27 (1992): 236. The view expressed in this particular article is typical of many law review pieces on the Court's decision in *Payne.* See, for example, Aida M. Alaka, "Victim Impact Evidence, Arbitrariness, and the Death Penalty: The Supreme Court Flipflops (Case Note) *Payne v. Tennessee,* 111 S.Ct. 2597 (1991)," *Loyola University of Chicago Law Journal* 23 (1992): 581–617; Michael Q. Berkeley, "What You Don't Know Can Kill You: The Rehnquist Court's Allowance of Unforeseeable Victim Impact Evidence in the Era of Disposable Precedent (Case Note) *Payne v. Tennessee,* 111 S.Ct. 2597 (1991)," *Wake Forest Law Review* 27 (1992): 741–68; K. Elizabeth Whitehead, "Mourning Become Electric: *Payne v. Tennessee*'s Allowance of Victim Impact Statements during Capital Sentencing Proceedings (Case Note) *Payne v. Tennessee,* 111 S.Ct. 2597 (1991)," *Arkansas Law Review* 45 (1992): 531–59.

32. I am indebted to Madelaine Adelman for pointing out that in her comments, Bendor also reiterates the Court's traditional commitment to a strong distinction between reason and emotion, a distinction that has long been criticized by feminist legal scholars. For example, see Virginia Held, *Feminist Morality: Transforming Culture, Society, and Politics* (Chicago: University of Chicago Press, 1993).

sentencing decision. Thus, her argument effectively reiterates and reinforces the assumption that expressions of pain are capable of tran-
scending personal, cultural, and ideological boundaries in a way that
rational, moral, and legal arguments are not and, thus, may provide
shared grounds for judgment when these arguments cannot.[33]

A similar point is made when critics argue that victim impact evidence should not be allowed in court because defendants, when confronted with the testimony of their victims (broadly construed), will
catalog all of the abuses they have suffered in their own lives.[34] According to Martha Minow, for example, the classic rejoinder to victimhood
takes the form, "Don't blame me; I'm a victim too."[35] However, in so
saying, Minow inadvertently makes the point that everyone is or can be
identified as a victim. While she may intend to criticize the kind of psy-

---

33. In effect, victims' rights advocates argue that the victim must be placed on the
stand so that the intellectual arguments offered by the defense may be countered by the
spectacle of suffering that prompts human feeling and spurs people to respond according
to the dictates of an essential human moral sense. According to Jean-Jacques Rousseau,
human beings naturally feel compassion for people who are in pain and are instinctively
repelled by whatever causes this pain. Consequently, when a man sees another man in
agony, he will rush without reflection to the afflicted man's aid. Rousseau claims that the
first man does not think about what he is doing and does not have to be trained or otherwise educated to act. On the contrary, reason turns man inward into himself and separates him from everything that naturally troubles him or affects him.

> A fellow-man may with impunity be murdered under [a philosopher's] window,
> for the philosopher has only to put his hands over his ears and argue a little with
> himself to prevent nature which rebels inside him from making him identify him-
> self with the victim of the murder. The savage man entirely lacks this admirable tal-
> ent, and for want of wisdom and reason he always responds recklessly to the first
> promptings of human feeling. (101)

In other words, Rousseau claims that intellectual arguments overpower the capacity of
men to identify with one another and thus destroy the sense by which human beings recognize good and evil, right and wrong. This sense of pity is so strong in the state of nature
that it takes the place of laws, morals, and virtues. Pity does not make men perfect, but "it
will always dissuade a robust savage from robbing a weak child or a sick old man of his
hard-won sustenance" (101). See *A Discourse on Inequality* (1755), trans. Maurice Cranston
(London: Penguin, 1984).

34. It is interesting to note that most of these arguments object to victim impact evidence on the grounds that the defendant will be encouraged to produce this same kind of
evidence and use it to excuse or mitigate his crime. However, since *Lockett v. Ohio* (1978),
the defendant has effectively been permitted to explain to the court how he suffered during his life in hopes of persuading the judge and jury to be lenient in their sentencing
decision. See *Lockett v. Ohio*, 438 U.S. 586 (1978).

35. Martha Minow, "Surviving Victim Talk," *U.C.L.A. Law Review* 40 (1993): 1415.

chological material that is presented as mitigating evidence in capital trials, her criticism actually reveals that the experience of pain and suffering is terribly common. Of course, Minow is also implying that defendants will identify themselves as victims in order to escape blame for their actions. However, this suggestion only calls attention to the fact that claims to victimhood are difficult, if not impossible, to deny. Noting this herself, Minow argues that it is necessary to develop criteria by which to evaluate competing claims about victimization. Specifically, along with attention to structures of oppression, she calls for explicit normative standards for evaluating historical harms (1438).

These observations are not intended to indicate support of the Court's decision in *Payne*. I offer them only to clarify a possible explanation as to why the Court reversed itself on the obviously controversial issue of victim impact statements in the context of capital trials. Recall that, as Kennedy observes, again in *McCleskey v. Zant*, "One of the law's very objects is the finality of its judgments. Neither innocence nor just punishment can be vindicated until the final judgment is known" (832). As the highest court in the United States, the Supreme Court has to articulate the grounds of such final judgments in a pluralist society. In other words, the Court must discover a "sacred name" or an ideal that can serve in our society as an absolute. Our desire for such an absolute, one in whose name we may justify lethal acts of punishment, plays an important role in the history of the country's death penalty jurisprudence. This desire, as described by Nietzsche, is a desire for death.[36] However, the death desired is not the death of the convicted criminal. According to Nietzsche, we long for the death of life. The desire for an absolute upon which or with which to ground final judgments expresses a longing for a kind of existence, one that is opposed to existence in this world where life is shocking and unpredictable. In brief, we want a doctrine that will systematize and negate the vicissitudes of life. Understood in this context, the Court's decision in *Payne* is not as surprising as it is illuminating of the condition of modernity.

In the next section, I will construe expressions of pain and suffering as expressions of an ideal with which final decisions in a pluralist society may be justified.

---

36. Friedrich Nietzsche, *On the Genealogy of Morality* (1887), trans. Carol Diethe, ed. Keith Ansell-Pearson (Cambridge: Cambridge University Press, 1994).

The Authority of Pain

Universal and Particular Pain

In the context of a capital trial, expressions of pain and suffering are distinguished by the fact that they are both universal and particular at once. Consider the fact that the circumstances that give rise to pain are always particular. Whereas the cause may be a common daily event like a pin prick, the suffering of that pain occurs always and only in a particular person. What is more, the "quantity" of pain inflicted provides no certain measure of the "quality" of pain suffered. The amount of adversity a particular person faces does not neatly nor necessarily indicate how much pain he or she feels. While some people seem capable of withstanding incredible amounts of physical and psychological hardship, others seem to suffer terribly from the smallest affliction.[37]

Indeed, so "particular" is physical pain that some have suggested that it cannot really be expressed in words at all. In *The Human Condition*, Hannah Arendt claims that pain is one of the most intense feelings humans ever know but at the same time, one of "the most private and least communicable."[38] Because pain is so removed from "the world of things and men," she says, it does not, indeed cannot, assume an appearance there (51). Elaine Scarry echoes this argument in *The Body in Pain*, observing that pain is "to the individual experiencing it overwhelmingly present, more emphatically real than any other human experience, and yet is almost invisible to anyone else, unfelt, and

---

37. As there is no "objective" measure of suffering, critics of victim impact evidence argue that people who testify in death penalty cases may pretend to suffer more than they actually do so that the sentencing authority in the case will punish the defendant as severely as possible. The Court recognizes this aspect of suffering when it notes in *Booth v. Maryland* that the defendant "rarely would be able to show that the family members have exaggerated the degree of sleeplessness, depression, or emotional trauma suffered" (506). In addition, the Court points out that the family members may not always intend to misrepresent their suffering. While one person's sense of loss may be as great as another's, he or she may not be as willing or able to express it. As a result, his or her suffering may not be treated with the same respect as the suffering of a more eloquent survivor. Recognizing the strength of this argument, the Court refuses to permit victim impact evidence in capital trials. The Court's own observations are often repeated by critics of the Supreme Court's eventual decision to allow victim impact statements in capital trials. See, for example, Vivian Berger, "*Payne* and Suffering—a Personal Reflection and a Victim-Centered Critique," *Florida State University Law Review* 20 (1992): 21–65.

38. Hannah Arendt, *The Human Condition* (Chicago: University of Chicago Press, 1958), 50–51.

unknown."[39] Again reiterating a point that Arendt makes, Scarry says that pain is imperceptible to others because it, unlike any other state of consciousness, is not *of* or *for* anything in the external world and, therefore, cannot be objectified in language (5).

Nevertheless, pain and suffering are also experiences with which everyone is intimately familiar, and the assumption of the universality of the experience of pain has served as the premise of much moral and political philosophy.[40] This includes the philosophy of the Scottish Enlightenment from which the founders drew when they composed the Declaration of Independence and the Constitution of the United States.[41] For example, one of the tenets of David Hume's philosophy is that man is not a reasoning creature but a feeling one. According to Hume:

> The chief spring or actuating principle of the human mind is pleasure or pain; and when these sensations are remov'd, both from our thought and feeling, we are, in a great measure, incapable of passion or action, of desire or volition.[42]

Based on this observation, Hume tries to establish an ethics that does not depend upon abstraction and the kind of absolute certainty that exists only in pure logic and mathematics.

Similarly, Jeremy Bentham's philosophy of utilitarianism, though critical of the "moral sense" philosophy of people like Hume, argues that feeling governs human beings in all they do, in all they say, and in all they think. According to Bentham, pain is one of two "sovereign masters" to which human beings will always submit.[43] He famously claims that every effort we can make to throw off our subjection serves

---

39. Elaine Scarry, *The Body in Pain: The Making and Unmaking of the World* (Oxford: Oxford University Press, 1985), 51.

40. Indeed, unless one assumes that everybody can and does experience pain and suffering, the tone of Scarry's comments about the body in pain make little sense. For without this assumption there is no reason to accept the implicit starting point of her analysis, which is that those who torture should know better. See discussion of this point below.

41. See Garry Wills, *Inventing America: Jefferson's Declaration of Independence* (New York: Vintage, 1978).

42. David Hume, *A Treatise of Human Nature* (1739), ed. Ernest Mossner (London: Penguin Books, 1969), 625.

43. Jeremy Bentham, *An Introduction to the Principles of Morals and Legislation* (1822), ed. J. H. Burns and H. L. A. Hart (London: Athlone Press, 1970), 11.

but to demonstrate and confirm it. Bentham claims that human beings will always choose the course of action that reduces the amount of pain they have to suffer.

The unique status of pain is challenged, however, by the other sovereign master of which Bentham speaks: pleasure. Is not pleasure, too, a private experience with which everyone is intimately familiar? Might not pleasure serve just as well as pain to justify sentencing decisions? Pleasure does not, however, enjoy the same privilege as pain as a force in the political, legal, or moral imagination. Pleasure is too elusive and quixotic. In contemporary political philosophy, consider the example of John Rawls's theory of justice.[44] In Rawls's famous thought-experiment, behind the veil of ignorance individuals know nothing of their own social, legal, economic, or personal status. Rawls argues that individuals in this condition will always choose as principles of justice those principles which will assure them of the least painful existence should they find themselves one of the least advantaged members of society. Critics of Rawls's theory of justice argue that individuals are much more likely to take risks than Rawls would suggest, as the benefits of taking such risks would be so great should they turn out to be one of the most advantaged members of society.[45] These critics may be correct, but they do not challenge Rawls's basic assumption that the safest course of action is to prepare for pain and suffering. In their own terms, to stake one's life on pleasure is a risk, while pain is a safe bet.

Thus, pain may be perceived as at once a particular and a universal experience. When this is understood, survivors who testify to their suffering, both emotional and physical, appear to speak in simultaneously individual[46] and general terms. For this reason, the Supreme

---

44. See John Rawls, *A Theory of Justice* (Cambridge: Harvard University Press, 1971).

45. See T. M. Scanlon, "Rawls' Theory of Justice," in *Reading Rawls: Critical Studies on Rawls' "A Theory of Justice,"* ed. Norman Daniels (Stanford: Stanford University Press, 1989), 169–205.

46. Indeed, this is why victims have sought the right to testify during the sentencing phase of capital trials. Victims' rights advocates argue that the prosecution in a criminal trial does not represent the individual but the state. Consequently, the prosecution is not conducted in such a way as to best serve the memory or the interests of the unique individuals involved. In the courtroom and particularly in their testimony, victims' rights advocates argue, victims call attention to these interests and demand respect for the particularity of the experience of physical and emotional suffering to which they testify. See David L. Roland, "Progress in the Victim Reform Movement: No Longer the 'Forgotten Victim,'" *Pepperdine Law Review* 17 (1989): 35–58; George Nicholson, "Victims' Rights, Remedies, and Resources: A Maturing Presence in American Jurisprudence," *Pacific Law Journal* 23 (1992): 833 and n. 60.

Court may embrace pain as a sacred name. In a society where no super-natural authority or abstract formula of judgment enables people to articulate and apply general (moral) laws without concern that they are failing to respect the uniqueness of the situation and the particularity of the individuals involved, survivors of victims of horrible crimes testify about specific experiences to which judges and jurors may respond without concern that they are using their own personal values or cultural standards to judge others. In effect, the experiences to which survivors testify are at once their own and everyone else's. In their pain, survivors reveal grounds for judgment that people from different cultural backgrounds and all walks of life share.

Irrefutable Pain

As I noted earlier, the ability of everyone to identify with or as a victim is often grounds for criticism of the Court's decision in *Payne*. However, it is difficult to respond to Minow's call to establish explicit normative standards for evaluating competing claims about victimization as people providing victim impact evidence testify to their *feelings*. Indeed, this observation introduces a second reason for suggesting that the Supreme Court embraces pain and suffering as grounds for judgment when it decides that victim impact evidence may be permitted during the sentencing phase of capital trials. The experience of pain to which victims' surviving family members and loved ones testify cannot be refuted. Even expert witnesses who testify with great authority about some aspect of a case may be challenged or contradicted by other experts who disagree with them. By contrast, people who testify about their feelings introduce into the courtroom facts that can be neither verified nor denied. While it may be argued that the victims have to act consistently with their testimony, their actions neither definitively confirm nor deny the veracity of their experience.[47] As noted above, what survivors say does not refer to things or even states of affairs in the world. Consequently, it is difficult to show when, if at all, they are lying

---

47. The demand that victims act consistently with their testimony is most commonly expressed in cases where individuals seek legal redress for sexual harassment. In such cases, the finder of fact will focus on the plaintiff's behavior after the alleged harassment for evidence that the plaintiff was indeed victimized. Still, as widespread support for Anita Hill in the wake of the Clarence Thomas confirmation hearings attests, the public does not necessarily judge the veracity of reported harassment on the grounds of the "victim's" actions alone.

or otherwise misrepresenting the experiences of which they speak. This difficulty has practical implications for death penalty trials. For instance, defendants' lawyers will hesitate to attack survivors who testify against their clients during the sentencing phase because a brutal cross-examination might reflect badly on their clients and make them seem even more cruel and unsympathetic than they already do.[48] Indeed, the most the defense can hope to accomplish by questioning a victim's loved one is to cast doubt upon his or her character or the character of the victim him- or herself. In the final analysis, it cannot disprove what the loved one says about his or her emotional state or sense of physical well-being.[49]

However, the difficulty with which victim impact evidence is refuted is due not only to the defendant's limited ability to challenge what survivors say. This difficulty is also due to the authority with which survivors speak. As survivors are called on to testify only to their pain and suffering, they testify to what they alone can know and what they alone can know with a unique confidence. As Scarry observes in *The Body in Pain*, "[F]or the person in pain, so incontestably and unnegotiably present is it that 'having pain' may come to be thought of as the most vibrant example of what it is to 'have certainty'" (4).

Of course, Scarry also suggests that "hearing about pain" may exist as the primary model of what it is "to have doubt." But Scarry's whole analysis of pain is motivated by the observation that a person can be in the presence of another in pain and not even be aware of it.

---

48. This danger is noted often in arguments against the admissibility of victim impact evidence. See also *Booth v. Maryland*, 507. Simultaneously, the victims' rights movement is working to make it illegal to cross-examine such witnesses. According to the National Victim Center, victims and their family members need to be protected from "harassment." Thus, states like New York require that the defendant present written questions to the court, which the court may, if it chooses, put to the victim (N.Y. Crim. Proc. Law 380.50). See *1996 Victims' Rights Source Book*, 222.

49. In *A Treatise of Human Nature*, Hume observes:

Reason is the discovery of truth or falsehood. Truth or falsehood consists in an agreement or disagreement either to the *real* relations of ideas, or to *real* existence and matter of fact. Whatever, therefore, is not susceptible of this agreement or disagreement, is incapable of being true or false, and can never be an object of our reason. Now 'tis evident our passions, volitions, and actions, are not susceptible of such agreement or disagreement; being original facts, and realities, compleat in themselves, and implying no reference to other passions, volitions, and actions. 'Tis impossible, therefore, they can be pronounced either true or false, and be either contrary or conformable to reason. (510)

This is made clear when Scarry asks, "How is it that one person can be in the presence of another person in pain and not know it—not know it to the point where he himself inflicts it, and goes on inflicting it?" (12). This question presumes exactly that which is in doubt, the certainty of the pain of the other person. In her work on the conditions of the possibility of doubt in the face of pain, Scarry never suggests that the experience of pain itself is not true. Thus, I cite Scarry here in support of my claim that victim impact evidence may seem irrefutable not only because it cannot be denied, but also because it is presented with a powerful sense of surety.

When survivors speak of their pain in court, what they say is rendered even more certain by their personal proximity to death. In a society that recognizes no other universal or absolute truths, death is the only shared certainty. By virtue of the fact that they were close to the murder victim, survivors are identified as such and are then permitted to testify during the penalty phase of the convicted murderer's trial. Indeed, people who testify to the impact of a particular person's murder on their lives may be characterized as themselves victims of that murder. As we have already seen, in its *Payne* decision the Court defines the magnitude of a capital crime by its effects on family members and loved ones. The pain of which these people speak is therefore understood as part of the act for which the defendant must be punished. In short, when survivors speak, they may speak not only on behalf of the victim but *as* victims of the defendant's crime.

The principle of this substitution is clarified by a comment in *The Body in Pain*. In it, Scarry observes that often pain is used as a symbolic substitute for death. She attributes this substitution to "an intuitive human recognition that pain is the equivalent in felt-experience of what is unfeelable in death" (31). Similarly, Arendt suggests, "Pain [is] truly a borderline experience between life as 'being among men' *(inter homines esse)* and death" (51). Observing the intensity with which pain is felt, Arendt argues that the experience of pain deprives human beings of their feeling for all other experiences, and thus for those experiences that human beings share with one another. Both Arendt and Scarry suggest, then, that pain is death in life. Those who speak of their pain represent death to the living. In this light, people who testify to their pain may be understood to introduce into the court nothing other than an unknowable but undeniable universal to which judges and jurors may appeal to ground their absolute judgments. In a world deprived of God (as Camus puts it), pain remains to justify punishment.

The Cause of Pain

A third feature of victim impact evidence is that what survivors say validates a beleaguered principle of causality at law. Survivors who testify to their pain during the penalty phase of a capital trial implicitly assume and explicitly reiterate the view that an individual caused and thus may be held responsible for their suffering. Likewise, the criminal law in the United States is premised on the assumption that autonomous human agents are the causes of the events that disrupt the pattern of everyday life in an ordered society and may be held responsible at law for the consequences of their actions. In the United States, in order to be found guilty of a crime, the accused must have committed a "guilty act" or wrongful deed with criminal intent or a "guilty mind." Both elements must be present for an act to be recognized as a crime at law.

However, when a particular defendant is found guilty of committing a crime, it is still possible for the defendant to argue that he or she was not in full possession of his or her faculties at the time of the criminal act. Should there be any evidence of external conditions or internal limitations that made it particularly difficult for the defendant to stay in control, he or she is held responsible for the crime but is not considered as blameworthy as he or she might otherwise be.[50] As the kind of personal facts and psychological material introduced by the defense mitigate the crime to the extent that they show the limits under which the defendant was able to exercise his or her free will, critics charge that the presentation of such factors does nothing other than suggest that the defendant's actions were determined and they claim that if this view is adopted, people may not longer be held accountable for their actions at

---

50. The necessity of this kind of defense in a capital trial is explained by the Supreme Court in *Woodson v. North Carolina*, 428 U.S. 280 (1976). In *Woodson*, the Supreme Court holds that any capital system that precludes consideration of "mitigating circumstances" is unconstitutional. The Court claims that because death is qualitatively different from a sentence of imprisonment, there is a corresponding difference in the need for reliability in determination that death is the appropriate punishment for a particular defendant.

law.[51] Such criticisms seem perfectly warranted when death penalty opponents suggest that given enough time and money to investigate the circumstances of a defendant's life, no man or woman would ever be sentenced to death.[52]

In *Payne v. Tennessee*, the Court argues that victim impact evidence should be permitted in the courtroom during the penalty phase of a capital trial in order to counter the force of the defendant's mitigating evidence. As Chief Justice Rehnquist claims in the majority opinion, "[J]ustice, though due to the accused, is due to the accuser also. The concept of fairness must not be strained till it is narrowed to a filament. We are to keep the balance true" (827).[53] This balance is preserved by allowing survivors to introduce a reality into the courtroom that otherwise is not available to the sentencing authority when it decides the defendant's fate: the pain and suffering of the victim's survivors. However, the nature of this "reality" begs the question of cause and effect. In brief, the effect points to a cause. By presenting to the court the certain effects of the defendant's actions, effects the defendant "produces," victim impact evidence reinforces the disparaged assumption that the defendant is the autonomous, rational, self-determining individual who caused these effects. Thus, victim impact evidence serves to protect the criteria with which the sentencing authority makes the decision to sentence a person to death. Of course, the Court itself does not explicitly make this point. However, the Court's justification for admitting victim impact statements during the penalty phase of capital trials reveals that the Court might embrace victim impact statements for this reason nevertheless.

The Court's justification for changing its position on the admissibility of victim impact evidence in capital cases is most clearly articulated by Justice Antonin Scalia in his dissent in *Booth v. Maryland* (1986). While the Court did not accept Scalia's argument in 1986, a few years later his reasoning was adopted as the Court's own. In his *Booth* dissent, Scalia claims:

---

51. For example, see Pamela Hediger, "*Mens Rea:* The Impasse of Law and Psychiatry," *Gonzaga Law Review* 26 (1990–91): 613–26.

52. Comment made by Craig Haney at a symposium on capital punishment at Arizona State University, Tempe, October 3, 1997.

53. Quoting Justice Benjamin Cardozo in *Snyder v. Massachusetts,* 291 U.S. 97, 122 (1934).

Many citizens have found one-sided and hence unjust the criminal trial in which a parade of witnesses comes forth to testify to the pressures beyond normal human experience that drove the defendant to commit his crime, with no one to lay before the sentencing authority the full reality of human suffering the defendant has produced—which (and *not* moral guilt alone) is one of the reasons society deems his act worthy of the prescribed penalty. (520)

Scalia here makes two points that the Court eventually adopts in its opinion in *Payne:* (1) criminal trials appear unjust because the defendant is allowed to present the jury with personal information supporting the argument for a sentence less than death; and (2) the crime for which the defendant is to be punished is defined in part by the suffering he or she produces, even if unintentionally. In this dissent Scalia also suggests that victims are uniquely capable of presenting the sentencing authority in a capital case with "the full reality of human suffering." Indeed, Scalia intimates that stories told by and about victims will lay before the trial court a reality that is otherwise missing, a reality that is explicitly associated with pain.

Of course, witnesses for the defendant in capital trials typically tell stories of extraordinary abuse and poverty. However, according to Scalia, these witnesses testify only to "pressures beyond normal human experience."[54] In other words, Scalia employs the vocabulary of pain exclusively for the survivors. In this way, he reserves for them alone the capacity to communicate the universal experience of pain, the experience to which Scalia refers as "the full reality of human suffering."

What is more, Scalia indicates that this reality is *produced* by the defendant. "Suffering" is endured by passive subjects. By contrast, "pressures" are experienced by active agents.[55] The defense wants to argue that the defendant's actions are, at least in part, the effects of other people's actions. Such an argument positions the defendant as a link in a chain of consequences originating with someone else. By using the word "pressures" rather than "suffering" to describe what the defendant feels, Scalia subtly characterizes the defendant as an autonomous, self-contained subject whose actions may be influenced but are not determined by external forces. The mechanical vocabulary

---

54. It is widely recognized that most, if not all, criminals on death row are victims of child abuse and poverty.

55. I am grateful to the copy editor of this piece for the formulation of this point.

employed not only dehumanizes the defendant but also puts him or her in the position of a person who can let off steam before violently erupting.[56] According to Scalia's account of human suffering, only victims feel it and only defendants cause it.

The certainty of the effects produced by the defendant's actions is taken up in Justice David Souter's concurring opinion in *Payne v. Tennessee*. In this opinion, Souter explicitly argues against critics who claim that victim impact evidence is irrelevant to the defendant's blameworthiness. According to such critics, the defendant can only be held responsible for what he or she knew at the time of the crime. In the case of *Payne v. Tennessee*, for example, the fact that Nicholas misses his mother and sister does not have any bearing on what the defendant deserves as punishment for having killed them and for having attacked Nicholas himself. As Payne tried to kill Nicholas, he could not possibly have known that the little boy would suffer in the wake of the murders. Souter disagrees with this argument. Specifically, he says:

> The fact that the defendant may not know the details of a victim's life and characteristics, or the exact identities and needs of those who may survive, should not in any way obscure the further facts that death is always to a "unique" individual, and harm to some group of survivors is a consequence of a successful homicidal act so foreseeable as to be virtually inevitable. (838)

Souter effectively argues that defendants in a capital trial can and should know, even before committing a violent crime, the loss that their victims' survivors will feel. Because human beings live in a "web of relationships and dependencies," when survivors take the stand and testify to their anguish, they do nothing more than render specific the common knowledge of the consequences of murder (839). And given that what survivors have to say is already generally understood, their particular comments should be not be excluded from capital trials.

However, in so arguing, Souter conflates the consequences of acts with actors' intentions. If these consequences are indeed "so foreseeable as to be virtually inevitable," how are they to be separated from the acts as such? When persons act, they must act with the knowledge

---

56. To dehumanize the defendant, prosecutors will also try to make him or her out to be a monster. See Austin Sarat, "Speaking of Death: Narratives of Violence in Capital Trials," *Law and Society Review* 27 (1993): 19–58.

that these consequences will be realized.[57] Ironically, this point is made in the context of a case in which the unintended and certainly unexpected failure of an act of homicide lead to consequences the defendant was supposed to anticipate.

In Souter's opinion then, the survivors play a central role in establishing the grounds upon which the criminal is ultimately defined as such and assigned responsibility for his or her crimes. Arguing backward from the experience of pain to which survivors testify, Souter establishes that the defendant acts with the knowledge that his or her actions will produce this pain.[58] Despite the obvious problems with this approach to determining responsibility at law, Souter assumes that the effects to which these individuals testify point to the presence of a causal agent, one that is autonomous, rational, and self-determining.[59] Evidence of suffering points to a culprit who alone may be held accountable at law for causing that harm.

Of course, criminals are not the only cause of human pain. Natural disasters, like hurricanes for example, produce devastating effects and incredible physical and emotional suffering for those who survive. However, natural disasters may not be held criminally responsible for what they do. Indeed, according to Walter Berns, we would never think to do so, as we cannot be angry at forces of nature. Berns's philosophy of anger elucidates how the experience of victimization may be conceived of as indicating the presence of a responsible criminal actor.

> Anger is expressed or manifested on those occasions when someone has acted in a manner that is thought to be unjust, and one of its bases is the opinion that men are responsible, and should be

---

57. Significantly, throughout his opinion, Souter, like Rehnquist in the majority opinion and the other justices who concur with it, cites *Tison v. Arizona*, 481 U.S. 137 (1987).

58. Evidence for the practice of this kind of deductive logic is supplied by Stephen L. Carter in an article about African-American victims of crime. Carter argues that American society does not recognize blacks as victims, and as a result of this lack of recognition, criminal acts committed against blacks are not treated as crimes. According to Carter, in this society the social reality of an act is determined by its effects. As Carter observes, "if there is no victim, there is no offense." See "When Victims Happen to be Black," *Yale Law Review* 97 (1988): 420–47.

59. For an extended discussion of these problems, see Jennifer L. Culbert, "Beyond Intention: A Critique of the 'Normal' Criminal Agency, Responsibility, and Punishment in American Death Penalty Jurisprudence," in *The Killing State: Capital Punishment in Law, Politics, and Culture*, ed. Austin Sarat (Oxford: Oxford University Press, 1999), 206–25.

held responsible, for what they do. . . . We can become angry with an inanimate object (the door we run into and then kick in return) only by foolishly attributing responsibility to it, and we cannot do that for long, which is why we do not think of returning later to revenge ourselves on the door. For the same reason, we cannot be more than momentarily angry with an animate creature other than man; only a fool or worse would dream of taking revenge on a dog. And, finally, we tend to pity rather than be angry with men who—because they are insane, for example—are not responsible for their acts. Anger, then, is a very human passion not only because only a human being can be angry, but also because it acknowledges the humanity of its objects: it holds them accountable for what they do.[60]

Pain in the Balance

Many critics have argued that by allowing victim impact evidence to be presented during the sentencing phase, the Court removes the sentencing authority's attention from the defendant and refocuses it on the victim at a key moment. In addition, they complain that by allowing the sentencing authority to focus its attention on the victim during the penalty phase, the Supreme Court paves the way for "mini-trials" on the victim's character.[61] Arguing as an advocate of victims' rights in her critique of the *Payne* decision, Vivian Berger claims that *Payne v. Tennessee* will allow the most profound insult—"decimation of the victim's memory"—to be added to the "ultimate injury" of death.[62] What is more, defense attorneys will be obliged to besmirch the deceased's memory whenever feasible or risk being held ineffective on appeal (51).

I suggest that the Supreme Court is willing to take this risk because of the security that survivors represent in the disorienting and ethically dangerous terrain of capital punishment. By identifying with the survivors, the sentencing authority can preserve its moral integrity and can claim to do justice in a pluralist society. While the Court does not say so explicitly, the chief justice suggests as much when he claims that hearing victim impact evidence will permit the judicial system to "keep the balance true" between the accused and the accuser.

60. Berns, *For Capital Punishment*, 153–54.
61. *Booth v. Maryland*, 507.
62. Berger, "*Payne* and Suffering," 50.

"Keeping the balance true" may not seem particularly controversial. However, in his *Payne* dissent, Stevens reminds the majority, "The victim is not on trial; her character, whether good or bad, cannot therefore constitute either an aggravating or a mitigating circumstance" (859). In her critique of the Court's *Payne* decision, Bendor elaborates on this point:

> The idea that there should be some sort of "balance" between the defendant's interests and individual victim's interests in a criminal sentencing proceeding contravenes the basic purpose of the proceeding itself. The majority in *Payne* ignores the fact that the purpose of a criminal sentencing proceeding is to make a decision about the defendant, not the victim. (240)

In other words, during the sentencing phase of a capital trial, there is no "balance" to be kept between the accused and the accuser. The accused has been found guilty and the only issue with which the court is concerned is his or her blameworthiness. In order to admit victim impact evidence, the Court has redefined the purpose of the sentencing proceeding. According to Stevens and critics of the Court, the majority has permitted the sentencing proceeding to be restructured in order to reinforce a bogus concept of fairness.

Stevens claims that the survivors' pain is a "non sequitur" in the sentencing proceeding. But according to Berger, logic has very little to do with the Court's opinion. In Berger's view, the decision is primarily aesthetic. Specifically she observes, "The post-*Payne* toleration of witnesses to the victim's life being permitted to share a podium with witnesses to the defendant's life produces a superficial symmetry pleasing to the public eye" (48). In other words, the "balance" to which Rehnquist refers as justification for the admission of victim impact evidence is an aesthetic conceit. In the context of a sentencing hearing that focuses on the details of the defendant's life, the appearance of survivors testifying to their pain is visually gratifying.

Berger is dismissive of the gratification this conceit brings. However, I believe this gratification should not be rejected too quickly. Aesthetics, and specifically the delight human beings take in order and harmony, is an essential element in the moral philosophy from which the Court may draw in its decision to permit victim impact statements in capital trials. Like philosophers of the eighteenth century, members of the Supreme Court are challenged to clarify the conditions of the possibility of passing judgment in this world, without referring to reason or other epistemological claims. Philosophers such as Hume find a solution to this challenge in the notion of "moral sense": "An action, or sentiment, or character is virtuous or vicious; why? Because its view causes a pleasure or uneasiness of a particular kind."[63] In the terms of this philosophy, the pleasure the public feels at the symmetry of the testimony provided by witnesses for the defendant and witnesses for the victim is evidence of the virtuousness of the Court's *Payne* decision. Indeed, the pleasure to which the "view" of this symmetry gives rise confirms its moral correctness. In *A Treatise on Human Nature,* Hume argues,

> We do not infer a character to be virtuous, because it pleases: we in effect feel that it is virtuous. The case is the same as in our judgments concerning all kinds of beauty, and tastes, and sensations. Our approbation is imply'd in the immediate pleasure they convey to us. (523)

In other words, Hume claims that we do not deduce from our feelings that the action, sentiment, or character under examination is either good or bad, right or wrong. Rather he claims that our feelings cannot be distinguished from the virtue or vice of that which we observe. Logic and rational measures of right and wrong do not apply; they pertain only in a realm of abstraction. In the real world, we feel justice when we see it.

Conclusion

What gives the public pleasure in the symmetry between the accuser and the accused is not simply the appearance or feeling of justice being done. While Hume argues that we need go "no further," that we need not inquire into the cause of our satisfaction, our pleasure is not as transparent as Hume suggests.[64] The pleasure we experience is com-

---

63. Hume, *Treatise of Human Nature,* 523.

64. Hume, *Treatise of Human Nature,* 523–24. Of course, I am not doing justice to Hume's philosophy here. For example, Hume is careful to observe that under the term *pleasure* we comprehend sensations that are very different from each other, and he notes that every sentiment of pleasure and pain is not necessarily that "peculiar" kind that makes us praise or condemn.

plex, particularly in the context of a legal trial in which death is a possible outcome.

I suggest that at least part of the pleasure of seeing both witnesses for the defendant and witnesses for the victim testify to their suffering is the meaning that this "balance" confers upon human suffering, and thereby upon the human condition. In the absence of an overarching principle or absolute to which to refer for sense and guidance in a multicultural, morally pluralist society, the survivor is embraced as a unique figure of authority with the power to liberate people from the chains of a well-meaning but paralyzing relativism. Ironically, however, this kind of liberation condemns us to a slave's existence. Let me explain.

The kind of existence of which I speak is described by Nietzsche in *On the Genealogy of Morality*. There, Nietzsche distinguishes between "nobles" and "slaves." Nobles relish the vicissitudes of life; they take pride and delight in the exercise of power and the fullness of existence. By contrast, slaves suffer from life. They are pessimistic and frightened. They also resent the nobles for the audacity of their spirit and for their lighthearted use of brute force. Yet slaves do not resent their suffering as much as they resent the fact that they can think of no justification, explanation, or affirmation for that suffering. In other words, they are most resentful when they are unable to give meaning to their pain. Nietzsche claims, "Man . . . does *not* deny suffering as such: he *wills* it, he even seeks it out, provided he is shown a *meaning* for it, a *purpose* of suffering" (127).

I do not mean to suggest that criminals lead more exalted or fulfilling lives than law-abiding citizens. Certainly, one would be hard-pressed to describe criminals' exercise of power as "noble," particularly in the Nietzschean sense of the word. I mean rather to suggest that a slave's life is one in which pain has to have meaning. In *The Genealogy of Morality*, Nietzsche shows how the weak save themselves from their sense of purposelessness by turning suffering into something to *will*, that is to say, something to choose, something to strive for. According to Nietzsche, this transvaluation of values is secured with the help of "the ascetic ideal," an ideal that posits an existence that is opposed to this world—the world of appearances, becoming, passing away, growth and death—in favor of another world in which life is constant, certain, and "real" (90). In the will to denounce this world in favor of that one, in short, in the will to will against the world and everything that belongs to it, human suffering comes to mean something. The act of negation or rejection of this world becomes the purpose or end of man. Consequently, "satisfaction is looked for and found in failure, decay, pain, misfortune, ugliness, voluntary deprivation, destruction of selfhood, self-flagellation and self-sacrifice" (91).

While no one may literally will the survivor's pain, everyone wants his or her suffering to have meaning. When a survivor testifies to his or her pain in a capital trial, it would be foolish, if not worse, to suggest that we do not see what we want to see: that suffering is not impotent, that pain is not ignored, that pain is not meaningless. By admitting victim impact evidence during the sentencing phase of a capital trial, the Supreme Court assures society that despite the fact that this world is plagued by random acts of brutal violence, there is another world in which the pain and suffering people endure as a result is not for nothing. In brief, the Court recognizes our pain and comforts us with the means of giving our suffering some sense.

However, as Nietzsche points out, the price of the kind of assurance the Court offers is bondage to an ideal that causes great pain and is itself ultimately doomed to be destroyed. In other words, the logic that compels the Court to embrace pain as a sacred name will eventually force the Court to acknowledge this figure as a false idol. In the end, the "victim" is, like all other absolutes, all too human. Some solace for critics of *Payne*.

The Problem of Pain and the Right to Die

Shai J. Lavi

Introduction: Pain and Modernity

Side by side with the development of medical knowledge, technologies, and institutions for solving the problem of pain,[1] there has been a growing interest in the social sciences and humanities with the emergence of pain as a modern problem.[2] Close attention has been given to historical changes in the understanding of pain and its treatment,[3] to the emergence of new forms of pain, especially chronic pain,[4] and to the varying cultural experiences of pain.[5] This paper aims to deepen and challenge this line of inquiry by examining the pain of dying as an extreme case of the problem of pain, and by focusing on the medical hastening of death as a uniquely modern solution to this problem.

The pain of dying and the hastening of death as its solution

The author wishes to thank Mark Antaki, Roger Berkowitz, Karl Shoemaker, and Sara Chinsky for their insightful remarks on early drafts of this paper, to Jill Colbert and Austin Sarat for drawing my attention to important if neglected aspects of the problem of pain, and to Hamutal Tsamir for her friendship in times of pain and pleasure.

1. For a comprehensive overview see Ronald Melzack and Patrick D. Wall, *The Challenge of Pain* (London: Penguin Books, 1982).

2. See, for example, Ivan Illich, *Medical Nemesis: The Expropriation of Health* (New York: Pantheon Books, 1976); and Mary-Jo DelVecchio Good et al., *Pain as Human Experience: An Anthropological Perspective* (Berkeley and Los Angeles: University of California Press, 1992).

3. Martin S. Pernick, *A Calculus of Suffering: Pain, Professionalism, and Anesthesia in Nineteenth-Century America* (New York: Columbia University Press, 1985); and Roselyne Rey, *The History of Pain* (Cambridge: Harvard University Press, 1998).

4. For example, R. Hilbert, "The Acultural Dimensions of Chronic Pain: Flawed Reality Construction and the Problem of Meaning," *Social Problems* 31, no. 4 (1984): 365.

5. M. Zoborowski, *People in Pain* (San Francisco: Jossey-Bass, 1969).

expose—more than any other encounter with pain—the growing intolerance of modern society to bodily suffering, and the uniquely modern ambition to not only overcome pain, but to annihilate it altogether. Standing at the intersection of death and pain, medicine and law, this paper asks: Why has the pain of dying become a problem for us, and how has the active hastening of death, implied in the quest for a "right to die," become its solution? What can we learn about pain and its place in the modern world from the way in which it has become so unbearable that death is sought as a refuge from life?

This paper is based on the argument that the struggle over the right to die is more than an attempt to grant individuals the abstract freedom to end their life. Rather, the right to die should be seen in the medical context in which it arises, and primarily as a solution to the problem of pain in dying. This is perhaps most notable with regard to the right to physician-assisted suicide. Research has shown that the primary reason for patients' wish to hasten their death is either the pain they are currently suffering, or the fear of the pain awaiting them in the future.[6] The medical hastening of death includes, in addition to physician-assisted suicide, the passive withholding of medical treatment, and its active withdrawal. By exploring these different forms of hastened death, this paper inquires into one of the more extreme confrontations of law and medicine with the problem of pain. While there are clearly other legal and moral justifications for hastening death,[7] the central role of pain in these decisions cannot be denied.

That pain and in particular the pain and suffering of dying patients has become a major concern among medical practitioners (and society

---

6. Kathleen Foley, "The Relationship of Pain and Symptom Management to Patient Requests for Physician-Assisted Suicide," *Journal of Pain and Symptom Management* 6, no. 5 (1991): 289.

7. From a legal point of view, the most common justification for hastening death is the autonomy of the patient. According to an old common-law tradition and the more contemporary interpretation of constitutional law, patients have the right to refuse any kind of medical treatment, even when such treatment is necessary for maintaining their life. Autonomy, however, in this context is an insufficient justification. It does not explain why the patient would wish to express her autonomy in this way, nor does it explain why the state's interest in preserving life would not supersede individual autonomy. Moreover, the autonomy of the patient cannot justify the active involvement of another party, the physician, in hastening death. Finally, there are many cases in which the wish of the patient cannot be determined, as in the case of patients in a persistent vegetative state.

Another justification for hastening death is grounded in the so-called right to die with dignity. Yet, dignity is a vague and indeterminate concept. Analysis shows, however, that an important aspect of dying with dignity, and perhaps the most important one, is control over one's body and over bodily pain and suffering.

at large) in recent years requires little proof. The emergence of numerous pain clinics, research projects, and pain societies dedicated to solving the problem of pain attest to this phenomenon, as does the rise of legal and medical solutions to the problem of pain in the form of right-to-die practices, such as physician-assisted suicide. However, current attempts in both medical and sociological literature to understand the origins and peculiarities of the modern encounter with pain fail to grasp the true meaning of the problem. It is almost as if the mere fact of the suffering body can account for both the problem of pain and its extreme solution.

One prevailing explanation of the emergence of pain as a medical and legal challenge in recent decades is the rapid innovations of technology. The unleashed medical capacity to prolong life by intrusive and extraordinary measures is often rightfully charged with being blind to the suffering of the patient, so that the prolonging of life becomes a prolonging of pain. Significant changes in the causes of death have also been offered as a reason for the growing concern with the pain of the dying. Patients today die more often from slow and painful killers such as heart disease, cancer, and AIDS, than from the swift and relatively painless ailments of the nineteenth century such as influenza, cholera, and tuberculosis. Under these new circumstances of death and dying, so the argument goes, there is an ever-growing need for new solutions to the problem of pain.

There is little doubt that medical and technological advances have indeed revolutionized the experience of dying, resulting in a prolonged and at times highly painful death. But the problem of pain in dying, as we shall see, predates these developments and can be traced back to the end of the nineteenth century, long before such changes took place.[8] The problem of pain, therefore, cannot be explained by the fact that dying has become more painful, a claim that in itself is highly questionable.[9] The problem of pain is not its intensity.

---

8. An enlightening survey of the history of euthanasia debates can be found in Ezekiel J. Emmanuel, "The History of Euthanasia Debates in the United States and Britain," *Annals of Internal Medicine* 121, no. 10 (1994): 793.

9. The argument that in our modern civilization there is an increased sensitivity to pain is not uncommon. Already in 1892 an article in a leading medical journal claimed, "Civilized man has of will ceased to torture, but in our process of being civilized we have won, I suspect, intensified capacity to suffer. The savage does not feel pain as we do: nor as we examine the descending scale of life do animals seem to have the acuteness of pain-sense at which we have arrived." Weir S. Mitchell, "Civilization and Pain," *Journal of the American Medical Association* 18 (1892): 108.

Another common explanation for the growing intolerance to pain is that not pain itself, but our perception of it, has made the pain of dying such an unbearable experience. Thus, the growing sensitivity to pain is another instance of the "civilizing process" by which Western societies have become less comfortable with extreme experiences in general, and pain in particular.[10] This sensitivity is perpetuated, since the avoidance of pain turns it into a rare experience, which in its turn leads to a higher sensitivity when it is encountered. But even if we have become more "civilized" in our attitude toward pain, this does not solve our problem, it merely begs it. Why have we become so sensitive to pain? Our growing sensitivity to pain is not what has made pain into a problem. If anything, the reverse is true. The perceived intensification of the pain of dying is the consequence, and not the ground, of pain's becoming a moral, medical, and legal problem.

Both these lines of argument are highly questionable. The problem of dying cannot be reduced neither to the growing intensity of pain, nor to an increased sensitivity to suffering. Nevertheless, taken together these views capture the prevailing understanding of the problem of pain and, as we shall see, determine the approach the courts take in deciding constitutional questions regarding the right to die. The first part of this paper is dedicated to unpacking the ways in which this commonsensical calculus of pain underlies some of the leading judicial decisions regarding end of life treatment.

In an attempt to deepen our understanding of the problem of pain and the hastening of death as its solution, the paper will move away from this commonsensical understanding of pain to a more radical and historically informed conceptualization of the problem. In the second part of the paper, the historical origin of the problem of pain in dying will be discussed. It is at the end of the nineteenth century, in the context of the medical treatment of the dying patient, that pain appears for the first time as utterly senseless. This happens at the very same time that the solution—hastening the death of dying patients—is first proposed. It is this senselessness that is central to understanding how the pain of dying became a modern problem.

Finally, in the third part of the paper, we shall return to the courts and the laws governing the practices of hastening death. Here we will see that even the decisions made by the courts cannot be understood on

10. Norbert Elias, *The Civilizing Process*, trans. Edmund Jephcott (New York: Pantheon, 1982).

the basis of a simple calculus of pain. Both the problem of pain and the extreme solution of hastened death will be reinterpreted in light of the understanding of pain that was developed in the previous section. It is here that a question will be raised about the price to be paid for the contemporary attempt to eradicate the experience of pain.

The Calculus of Pain: A Judicial Common Sense

In the summer of 1997, the Supreme Court of the United States refused to recognize a constitutional right to physician-assisted suicide.[11] In her concurring opinion Justice O'Connor wrote, "Death will be different for each of us. For many, the last days will be spent in physical pain and perhaps the despair that accompanies physical deterioration and a loss of control of basic bodily and mental functions. . . . I join the Court's opinions because I agree that there is no generalized right to 'commit suicide.' But respondents urge us to address that narrower question whether a mentally competent person who is experiencing great suffering has a constitutionally cognizable interest in controlling the circumstances of his or her imminent death."[12] O'Connor, along with the other judges, rejects the right to physician-assisted suicide not because dying is not as painful as it seems, but only because there are other ways for relieving such pain. O'Connor's suggestive allusion to a "right to control the circumstances of imminent death," while not directly addressing the problem of pain, has led one scholar to conclude that though the Court rejected the right to physician-assisted suicide, it affirmed a right to die a painless death.[13]

While the most recent right-to-die decisions clearly emerge in response to the problem of pain, the earlier cases seem to have very little to do with this problem. In fact most of these early cases, such as the well-known Quinlan case, dealt with patients who were not suffering from pain at all.[14] Karen Quinlan was a twenty-two-year-old woman who, on the night of April 15, 1975, fell into a state of unconsciousness. She was diagnosed as suffering from an irreversible comma, and it was believed that her life could only be maintained by the help of life-sus-

---

11. *Washington v. Glucksberg*, 521 U.S. 702 (1997); *Vacco v. Quill*, 521 U.S. 793 (1997).

12. *Washington v. Glucksberg*, 736.

13. Robert Burt, "The Supreme Court Speaks: Not Assisted Suicide but a Constitutional Right to Palliative Care," *New England Journal of Medicine* 337 (1997): 1234.

14. *In re Quinlan*, 70 N.J. 10 (1976).

taining machinery. Karen's parents, both Catholic believers, viewed the medical treatment as a use of extraordinary and futile means to prolong her life. Following their religious convictions, they asked that she be disconnected from the machine. The Supreme Court, granting Mr. Quinlan's request to be appointed as guardian, ordered the hospital to withdraw life support treatment. Karen did not die immediately. Her tragic life came to an end only a decade later. For current purposes, it is important to remember that Karen was not in pain while connected to the machines and, as the Court pointed out, she was unresponsive to pain of any kind, even deep pain.

From 1976 to 1985, the substantive issue presented to most state supreme courts concerned the withdrawal or withholding of respirators and other medical treatment from terminally ill, incompetent patients.[15] With one important exception, to be discussed later, these cases did not explicitly raise the problem of pain. The courts justified their decisions on the basis of the principle of self-determination expressed by the will of the patient, or his surrogate in cases in which the patient could not express his own wish. And yet, even these cases, which seem to have little to do with pain, are closely tied to the problem of pain, as we will see later.

The unbearable suffering of the dying patient captured the courts' attention in the 1985 case of Claire Conroy.[16] The guardian of an incompetent patient sought permission to remove a nasogastric feeding tube from an eighty-four-year-old bedridden woman with serious and irreversible physical and mental impairments and limited life expectancy. This request was brought before the Supreme Court of New Jersey, the same court that almost a decade earlier decided the well-known Quinlan case. Unlike Quinlan, the court in Conroy established a standard for withdrawing life-sustaining treatment, which was not based on reconstructing the subjective wish of the patient, but exclusively on her objective condition. The court held that recurring, unavoidable, and severe pain is in itself a sufficient reason for withdrawing all medical treatment and hastening death. The question arises: On what basis did the court make this decision? What is the logic of pain according to which the court found suffering so unbearable, that death was preferred over life?

---

15. Henry Glick, *The Right to Die: Policy Innovation and Its Consequences* (New York: Columbia University Press, 1992).

16. *In the Matter of Conroy*, 98 N.J. 321 (1985).

The explanation offered by the court is at once commonsensical and striking. The court justified the withdrawal of life-sustaining machinery on the basis of a remarkably crude calculus of pain. On one side of the equation stand the net burdens of a prolonged life, which consist of "the pain and suffering of [the patient's] life with the treatment less the amount and duration of pain that the patient would likely experience if the treatment were withdrawn." On the other side of the equation are the possible pleasures, which consist of "any physical pleasure, emotional enjoyment, or intellectual satisfaction that the patient may still be able to derive from life."[17]

One can extract the court's understanding of pain from this case and similar cases, in which the same logic is used.[18] Three basic principles guide the court's decision:

1. Pain is measured by its intensity and is understood primarily as a bodily sensation.
2. Pain and pleasure are opposites. Pain is to be diminished, pleasure increased.
3. Life is worth living only if the balance of pleasure outweighs that of pain.

This thematization closely resembles Bentham's approach to pain, and for this reason, I will refer to it as the Benthamite calculus of pain and pleasure.[19] In the court's application of the Benthamite calculus of pain, the dual understanding of the problem of pain as intensity and sensitivity comes into play. The court measures the pain suffered by the patient in terms of its intensity, while determining that a certain threshold of sensitivity exists beyond which pain should not be suffered.

Bentham's writings capture essential characteristics of the modern understanding of pain, which are still prevalent in today's law. While the scope of this work does not allow for a rigorous analysis of the Benthamite calculus of pain, some remarks may be helpful. Intensity, strictly speaking, is not the sole measure of pain, neither in Bentham's, nor in the court's opinion.[20] Indeed, Bentham discusses at least three

---

17. Ibid.

18. See, for example, *Brophy v. New England Sinai Hospital, Inc.*, 398 Mass. 417 (1986).

19. Jeremy Bentham, *An Introduction to the Principles of Morals and Legislation*, ed. J. H. Burns and H. L. A. Hart (London: Athlone Press, 1970).

20. Ibid., 38.

other dimensions of pain: duration, certainty and propinquity. Nevertheless, there is a sense in which the intensity of pain captures its Benthamite nature better than the other dimensions. It manifests an essential feature of any calculus of pain, the notion that pain can be measured.[21] Intensity seems to be the best measure of pain, and indeed one may loosely speak of pain being "more intense" the longer it lasts, and the more certain and frequent it is.[22]

Another point is that for Bentham pain is not primarily a bodily sensation. Rather, pain like pleasure is an affective category, one relating to emotions. This becomes clear when Bentham lists the different types of simple pains, including the pains of privation, the pains of enmity, the pains of an ill name, and so on, the pains of the senses being only one among a dozen such categories.[23] This broader understanding of pain is all but lost in the course of the medicalization of pain, in which bodily pain emerges as an "autonomous" experience, divorced from all other human experiences of suffering.

During the twentieth century, the medical profession developed not only the technologies to master pain, but also the language to understand it. To speak of a medicalization of pain, however, is not to argue that physicians have developed a monopoly on expertise. Rather, the medicalization of pain has created a language for thinking about pain, which has proliferated among nonexperts, in such a way that

---

21. Ronald Melzack, a highly respected authority on pain and coauthor of the pathbreaking "Gate Control Theory of Pain," wrote, "If the study of pain in people is to have a scientific foundation, it is essential to measure it. If we want to know how effective a new drug is, we need numbers to say that the pain decreased by some amount" (Melzack and Wall, *The Challenge of Pain,* 37).

22. Empirical evidence of a similar point can be found in an article from 1976, which argues that the most salient dimension in self-reported pain is its intensity. Carole A. Baily and Park O. Davidson, "The Language of Pain: Intensity," *Pain* 2 (1976): 319. A decade later Melzack writes, "Until recently, the methods that were used for pain measurement treated pain as though it were a single, unique quality that varies only in intensity" (Melzack and Wall, *The Challenge of Pain,* 37). While Melzack and his colleagues have reintroduced other dimensions of pain, Elaine Scarry has correctly pointed out that "when we attribute 'intensity' to something (which we consistently do with pain . . .) we usually in part mean that one dimension has become dominant. . . . One might say that if pain had a goal, it would be to be felt and known exclusively in its intensity. Those people working to make recognizable its other attributes are working against its insistent, self-isolating intensity, and therefore against pain itself." *The Body in Pain: The Making and the Unmaking of the World* (New York: Oxford University Press, 1985), 327.

23. Bentham, *Principles of Morals,* 42.

judges too can perform the medical calculus of pain.[24] The medical understanding of pain has been fused into the Benthamite calculus of pain so that pain in both the medical and legal context is, today, first and foremost a bodily sensation. This transformation of pain becomes evident when pain is compared to pleasure. While the court is still able to distinguish between different qualities of pleasure—physical, emotional, and intellectual—the only dimensions of pain are amount and duration, which are quantitative and closely related to the bodily aspect of pain.

It is this tendency to reduce pain to its bodily manifestations that is criticized in the opinion of Justice Handler in *Conroy*. Justice Handler, dissenting in part, raises questions as to whether the court's understanding of pain is defensible. He writes, "The presence of significant pain in effect becomes the sole measure of such a person's best interest. 'Pain' thus eclipses a whole cluster of other human values that have a proper place in the subtle weighing that will ultimately determine how life should end." Handler lists some of the nonphysical dimensions of suffering: "[S]ome people abhor dependence on others as much, or more than they fear pain. Other individuals value personal privacy and dignity, and prize independence from others when their personal needs and bodily functions are involved. Finally, the ideal of bodily integrity may become more important than simply prolonging life at its most rudimentary level."[25]

Justice Handler harbors serious doubts as to the "justice, efficacy and humaneness" of the standard set by the court. And yet the extent to which his view departs from the Benthamite calculus is by no means clear. While the sense of pain is broadened to include other forms of suffering that are not exclusively physical, the emphasis remains on the careful weighing and measurement of pain and pleasure. Indeed, one of Handler's objections to limiting the standard to physical pain is the difficulty of measuring it, since "health care providers frequently encounter difficulty in evaluating the degree of pain experienced by a patient."[26]

---

24. By the same token, physicians employ the language of law to speak of pain, as the following quote suggests: "We are appalled by the needless pain that plagues so many people. . . . Every human being has a right to freedom from pain" (Melzack and Wall, *The Challenge of Pain*, x).

25. *In the Matter of Conroy*, 394–96.

26. Ibid.

It is precisely this claim to knowledge that raises a very important question, one that has been mistakenly referred to as the epistemological problem of pain.[27] How can pain, whether physical or emotional, whether measured scientifically or not, be known to any one but the suffering patient herself? Given the subjective character of the experience of pain, how can pain be measured, and more generally, how can it be known to others? Pain, as we know, leaves no traces in the objective world and perhaps more than any other emotion or sensation lies solely within the private world of the sufferer.[28] While intense pain may become the only reality known to the suffering patient, it is always a questionable reality for those surrounding him. How, then, can judges base their decision to hasten the death of a patient on her intolerable suffering, when such suffering cannot be known to them?[29] The question is not only whether one should trust self-reported pain, but also how the pain of a dying patient, like Claire Conroy, can be evaluated when even self-reporting is impossible?

The Benthamite model of pain seems to leave us with a paradox.[30] On the one hand, pain is a subjective experience and therefore can be known only to the person suffering from it. On the other hand, pain can and should be calculated according to objective standards known to both the medical and the legal profession. How is it that the ephemeral existence of pain has become so real for us that today pain is not only a great source of anxiety, but also the ultimate grounds for medical and legal end-of-life decision making? While the so-called epistemological problem of pain is not central to this inquiry, some preliminary attempts to redefine this problem will emerge in the process of rethinking the Benthamite understanding of pain.

---

27. Perhaps the most influential representative of this approach to the problem of pain has been Elaine Scarry. Scarry speaks of the inexpressibility of physical pain and raises the epistemological problem of pain and its political consequences. The following discussion will raise serious doubts as to the validity of Scarry's representation of pain.

28. Love, fear, ambivalence, hunger, and all other interior states, but for pain, have referential contents. Pain, according to Scarry, is unique in this way: "It is not *of* or *for* anything" (*The Body in Pain*, 5).

29. The same question is raised by physicians regarding the administration of pain relief medication. They fear that giving such medication when unnecessary may lead to addiction, and that patients who are already drug abusers may take advantage of the situation.

30. While Scarry's approach to pain differs from Bentham's, together they capture our commonsensical and paradoxical understanding of pain as both calculable and subjective.

In what follows I would like to take to task the Benthamite under-standing of pain, and the justification (and explanation) it offers for the hastening of death as a solution to the problem of pain. The problem of pain cannot be encapsulated in a simple calculus of pain, nor is death the rational conclusion of such a calculus. To understand why the Ben-thamite calculus of pain does not get to the heart of the matter, I will turn to the moment in history in which the pain of dying first became a problem, and the hastening of death its preferred solution.

The legal understanding of pain will serve both as the point of departure and the final destination of this journey. Such a journey, however, cannot take place solely within the confines of the legal realm. For the law the pain of dying has become first and foremost a medical problem, and it is within this medical world that the modern problem of pain can most clearly be seen. Only after making the move from the commonsensical understanding of pain to the historical roots of the challenge of pain within the medical world will we return to reassess the place of pain in the legal realm.

The nineteenth-century medical discourse on pain and dying is important not only because it is the moment in which this problem first emerges in the modern scene. This early discussion of pain is signifi-cant because it takes place at a liminal stage in the development of med-icine as a science. While it encompasses the basic medical approach to pain that will persist throughout the twentieth century, it is formulated in a prescientific, almost metaphysical language that will soon be dis-carded. It is precisely at this historical moment that the metaphysical underpinning of the modern attitude toward pain can most clearly be accounted for.

The Emergence of the Modern Problem of Pain

It would be far from the truth to claim that the problem of pain and the solution of hastened death are uniquely modern. The idea that pain may become so unbearable that death is sought as a refuge from life is not novel. Zeno, the Stoic founder, committed suicide in old age prompted by the agonizing pain of a broken finger. Seneca, the great Roman orator, recommended "to free the struggling soul [from the use-less body], a little before the final debt is due, lest, when it falls due, one may be unable to perform the act." Nevertheless, even for the latter, the most enthusiastic advocate of suicide in ancient times, it was not pain as such that justified death. As he confessed, "I will not raise my hand against myself on account of pain, for so to die is to be conquered. But I know that if I must suffer without hope of relief, I will depart, not through fear of the pain itself, but because it prevents all for which I would live."[31]

The modern reincarnation of hastening death as a solution to the problem of pain in dying can be found in a short essay entitled "Euthanasia," published in 1870 by Samuel D. Williams. Williams, a nonphysician, advocated the use of chloroform not just to relieve the pain of dying, but to intentionally end the life of patients suffering from a hopeless and painful illness. Williams was the first in the modern context to openly propose the administration of lethal drugs as a just and routine solution to the agonies of dying.[32] Williams's proposal would probably have been forgotten were it not for the attention it drew from the medical profession and the controversy it aroused. Whether supporting the proposal or bitterly condemning it, the medical profession shared Williams's concern with the suffering of the dying patient.

Strictly speaking Williams was not the first to offer euthanasia to dying patients. Throughout the latter half of the nineteenth century euthanasia was quite commonly practiced among medical doctors, though the word carried quite a different sense. For most nineteenth-century physicians euthanasia denoted the ordinary treatment offered to dying patients, primarily the relieving of their pain, short, however, from taking their lives. It is in this ordinary practice of euthanasia (which is closer to the literal sense of euthanasia, good death) that we may find the origin of the modern problem of pain, as well as the medical solution offered to solve this problem.

Quite contrary to what one would assume, the problem of pain in dying during the nineteenth century had little to do with either the intensity of pain suffered by dying patients, or with the growing sensibility of patients to pain. In 1887 William Munk, a British physician, published his book *Euthanasia: or, Medical Treatment in Aid of an Easy Death*.[33] The main argument of the book is striking for anyone familiar

---

31. Derek Humphry and Ann Wickett, *The Right to Die: Understanding Euthanasia* (New York: Harper and Row, 1986).

32. Ezekiel J. Emmanuel, "The History of Euthanasia Debates in the United States and Britain," *Annals of Internal Medicine* 121, no. 10 (1994): 793.

33. William Munk, *Euthanasia or, Medical Treatment in Aid of an Easy Death* (New York: Arno Press, 1887).

with the modern process of dying. The dying, Munk claims, suffer no pain. "The process of dying and the very act of death is but rarely and exceptionally attended by those severe bodily sufferings, which in popular belief are all but inseparable from it."[34]

Munk did not hold an idiosyncratic belief. In fact, most physicians of the time shared his opinion that death was not painful. Since no one who had completed the process of dying could report back, the only reliable evidence came from those who faced death but eventually recovered. And indeed, to support the claim that dying is painless, a new genre of near-death experiences developed. The purpose of such accounts was to prove that those who faced death but were saved at the last moment did not suffer any pain.

One case, told in detail by Munk and others, is the story of Admiral Beaufort, who as a youngster fell overboard of a ship in Portsmouth harbor. Unable to swim, he was soon exhausted by his struggles and sank below the surface. "From the moment that all exertion had ceased," recalled the admiral, "a calm feeling of the most perfect tranquility superseded the previous tumultuous sensations—it might be called apathy, certainly not resignation, for drowning no longer appeared to be an evil. I no longer thought of being rescued, nor was I in any bodily pain." Fortunately, for him, after two long minutes he was saved. However, he recalled, "instead of being absolutely free from all bodily pain, as in my drowning state, I was now tortured by pain all over me."[35] As a rule, concludes Munk, the urgent symptoms of disease subside when the act of dying really begins: A "pause in nature, as it were, seems to take place."[36]

Besides anecdotal evidence, there were more scientific grounds for the claim that dying was painless. During the nineteenth century a new understanding of the dying process developed, claiming a common mechanism to all forms of death, whether natural or not. Important distinctions between the modes of dying were not overlooked, but the basic structure of dying had to transcend such distinctions. Whether caused by heart, lung, or brain failure, the underlying structure of dying remained the same. The previously dominant approach that dying could be accompanied by an excess of stimulation as much as by

---

34. Munk, *Euthanasia*, 7–8.
35. Ibid., 12–13.
36. Ibid., 20.

depletion was now revised with a theory that dying was a form of decay. All dying proceeded in a sequence of stages during which the body gradually lost its vital powers. The age-old analogy between death and sleep transformed in a very telling manner: not only natural death, but all modes of dying were ascribed the basic characteristics of sleep.[37] The analogy to sleep did not merely expand, but shifted. The crux of the analogy was not that death was akin to sleep, but rather that dying was a falling asleep. Both were unconscious and therefore painless.

Following this understanding of the dying process, other physicians at the turn of the century attempted to uproot the common belief that dying was painful. In the first decade of the twentieth century a leading physician, Sir William Osler, conducted more systematic research to prove a similar point.[38] In a study of the dying process of about five hundred patients, he reported that only ninety showed evidence of pain or distress. Of the five hundred, Osler claimed, "the great majority gave no sign one way or the other; like their birth, their death was a sleep and a forgetting."[39]

There is something very striking, not so much in these medical facts themselves, but in the picture of dying they attempt to portray. For Munk, Osler, and other physicians of the turn of the century, it became important to demonstrate that dying—popular beliefs and traditional wisdom notwithstanding—is by nature painless. To make such a bold claim, an ambiguous distinction had to be drawn between dying and illness, and the process of dying had to be confined to the very short span of time immediately preceding death. In order to understand the logic behind this highly dubious line of argumentation,[40] we

---

37. "All modes of death, with the exception of that from old age, may be regarded as more or less violent; but in considering their nature, we must not confound the last act of dying with the suffering which precedes it, and which is often no less when it terminates in recovery than in death, which equally relieves it; and as death in the usual acceptation of the word, from whatever cause it arises, consists in the loss of the sensorial functions alone, the act of dying is, in this respect, in all cases essentially the same." A. P. W. Philip, "On the Nature of Death," *Philosophical Transactions* 124 (1834): 167.

38. Shigeaki Hinohara, "Sir William Osler's Philosophy on Death," *Annals of Internal Medicine* 118 (1993): 638.

39. For an elaborate discussion of Osler's approach to death see Richard Golden, "Sir William Osler: Humanistic Thanatologist," *Omega* 36, no. 3 (1998): 241.

40. Such a representation of the dying process by the medical profession would surely be untenable today. As a contemporary physician referring to Osler's experiment has noted, "The last weeks and days of far more of my patients than Osler's one in five have been overfilled with a plethora of purgatory, and I have been there to see it." Sherwin Nuland, *How We Die* (London: Chatto and Windus, 1996).

ought first to consider the position these claims were attempting to counter. This medical position is worth exploring not for its highly questionable scientific findings, but for the glimpse it offers into the metaphysics underlying the medical approach to the pain of dying.

It was, no doubt, hard to challenge the opinion that dying is in fact painful, since such belief was deeply anchored in Christian metaphysics.[41] Pain in general and the pain of dying in particular have had a privileged place in Christian doctrine. The belief in the redeeming virtues of pain, the idea that suffering individuals were closer to Christ, that their anguish could be offered in penitence for earthly sins, or even that God put only his elected few through terrible trials were all recurrent themes throughout Church literature.[42] Moreover, the suffering of pain should not be relieved because it was important to maintain the patient's lucidity until his confession could be heard and until extreme unction was administered. This remains true, albeit for different reasons, in the Protestant tradition that maintained very high, even if less ritualistic, demands from the dying person.

All this became highly questionable in the course of the nineteenth century. An article from 1899, titled "The Natural Right To A Natural Death," already foreshadows our contemporary right-to-die debate. It reads, "The century which is about to close, and whose children we are, (for though we may share the life of the twentieth, its spirit we never can), has ennobled the world by bringing back the human mind to a more rational conception of God, and of his dealings with our race. One of the best results of this is that death has lost half its terrors for the present generation."[43]

Death had become a natural phenomenon; it had lost its enigmatic power. This is not to say that Americans stopped fearing the torments of hell, far from it, but from now on, death and dying could be viewed, and often were, as merely natural processes. Pain emerged at the deathbed in its raw form, distinguished from anguish and fear, guilt and sorrow. Modern man, dressed in the white coat of the medical physician, could accept neither the agonizing pain of eternal damnation, nor those of the deathbed. A new sense had to be given to pain or

41. The last article of life has often been characterized as "the mortal agony" and a "death struggle" accompanied by "the pangs of death." Maurice Maeterlinck, *Death* (New York: Dodd, Mead and Company, 1912).

42. For a rich historical account of attitudes toward pain, see Rey, *The History of Pain.*

43. Simeon E. Baldwin, "The Natural Right to a Natural Death," *St. Paul Medical Journal*, December 1899, 875, 886.

else pain had to be eradicated. The question the medical profession was facing was to what extent pain could still be justified, that is, have a place in the natural rather than supernatural world.

Even after pain was divorced from sin, evil, and punishment (what one may call, the de-Christianization of pain), it was still understood by the medical profession as necessary.[44] Pain had a positive role: it was seen as a warning or alarm signal that conveys the feelings of one's existence and alerts to the dangers challenging the body. It diverts one from a harmful lifestyle, warns of the approach of illness, and invites one to change before it is too late. Pain, in other words, has a telos.[45]

And yet, what is true of pain in general cannot be applied to the pain of dying. When one is dying, there is no longer any need to alert the body to its condition. Pain is intelligible only as a sign of life and hope. As we have seen in the case of the drowning admiral, pain recedes when dying begins, and returns only if and when recovery becomes possible. It is in this context that Munk's claim that dying itself cannot be painful should be understood. Pain became senseless in the double meaning of senselessness: it no longer made any sense for dying patients to suffer from pain, and dying patients were reported to sense no pain.

Munk's position is significant for our understanding of the modern problem of pain. Munk is not merely suggesting that the pain of dying is useless and therefore should be relieved; rather according to nature pain in dying is always already relieved. His argument is, in other words, ontological rather than moral. Or more accurately, his medical prescription that pain in dying should be relieved is based on the ontological premise that pain in dying is unnatural, therefore unnecessary, and can be relieved.

While medicine at the turn of the century rejected the Christian metaphysics of pain and dying, physicians at the turn of the century were actually proposing their own theology. Pain had to have a purpose; without one it could not be justified, and hence it could not exist. Unjustified pain was an enigma that carried its own rituals. The pain of

---

44. Donald Caton, "The Secularization of Pain," *Anesthesiology* 62 (1985): 493.

45. Melzack and Wall offer a more elaborate discussion of the purpose and value of pain and list three related functions of pain: first, pain that occurs before serious injury and is meant to prevent further injury; second, pain that is meant to teach one to avoid injurious objects or situations; third, pain after the injury designed to set limits on activity and enforce inactivity and rest (*The Challenge of Pain*, 11).

dying became senseless, but this did not mean that physicians remained powerless in the face of pain. On the contrary, they were called to duty—the duty of annihilating pain. Pain became senseless precisely because the only sense that it had was given to it by the medical machinery aimed at annihilating it.

The problem of pain in dying as perceived by most physicians around the turn of the twentieth century was not its intensity but its intelligibility, not increased sensitivity but diminished sensibility. The problem was how to make sense of its existence, and consequently how to reconcile the well-established medical claim that dying was painless with the occasional existence of pain in dying. Munk explains that while it is true that dying by nature is painless, dying may become painful because of the occurrence of physiological or pathological conditions, which precede or accompany it. The role of the physician is to assure that any such suffering, which is always external and accidental to the dying process, is mitigated. Munk offers several methods for overcoming pain, but clearly the most effective is opium, which, in his eyes, is "worth all the rest of the *materia medica*."[46]

Throughout the twentieth century, relieving the dying patient from the terrible torments of the deathbed has become not only the duty of the medical profession, but its true calling. In the words of Albert Schweizer, "We must all die. But that I can save [a person] from days of torture, that is what I feel as my great and ever new privilege. Pain is a more terrible lord of mankind than even death himself."[47]

Moreover, the reality of pain has changed since the days of Munk and Osler. The problem of the senselessness of pain has become ever more pressing, as the prevalence of chronic pain among dying patients rises. Chronic pain is a type of pain that "persists after all possible healing has occurred or, at least, long after pain can serve any useful function."[48] In other words, chronic pain is no longer simply a symptom of injury or disease, but becomes a pain *syndrome*—a medical problem in its own right. This transformation of pain from a mere symptom reflecting an underlying pathological condition to a syndrome with no external reference or purpose has made the pain of the dying patient ever

---

46. Munk, *Euthanasia*, 73.

47. Quoted in Munk, *Euthanasia*, v. The birth of the pain clinic and the hospice, along with the developments of pain control techniques in psychology, physiology, and clinical medicine, are manifestations of this growing concern.

48. Melzack and Wall, *The Challenge of Pain*, 36.

less tolerable. The purposelessness of any pain accompanying the dying process is today reinforced by the pointlessness of all chronic pain, the most common pain accompanying the dying process.

We are now ready to reassess the modern problem of pain. The reason why the pain of dying has become intolerable is not because pain has become more intense, nor because we have become more sensitive to it. Rather, the problem of pain in modern times is its senselessness. Pain is no longer tolerable because it can no longer be justified in terms of Christian metaphysics, or in the language of modern science. Furthermore, despite the obvious differences between modern medicine and Christian dogma, the two share the notion that pain, in its essence, is not only the opposite of pleasure, but like pleasure, is part of what it means to be a living human being. The lack of pain is a sign of death. Finally, it is not that life is unworthy living if the balance of pain outweighs that of pleasure, as the Benthamite calculus would have us think, but that pain, now no longer necessary, cannot be justified, and the pain of dying—the pain of life—is rejected in favor of a peaceful death.

The Calculus of Pain Revisited

Having gained a better understanding of the problem of pain, it is time to return to the courts and revisit our commonsensical understanding of pain. To accomplish this I will reevaluate the Benthamite approach in light of the deeper, more radical understanding of pain we have arrived at. To be sure, I am not proposing an alternative account of pain, but rather one that both underlies and is concealed by our commonsensical understanding.

The case of Saikewicz[49] reveals that the problem of pain is far from being a mere calculus of pleasure and suffering. Joseph Saikewicz was a sixty-seven-year-old, with an I.Q. of ten and a mental age of approximately two years and eight months. He was, as the court put it, profoundly mentally retarded. Saikewicz was at the time suffering from acute leukemia, and the only treatment that could save his life was chemotherapy. The question before the court was whether the appointed guardian's decision not to treat Saikewicz was indeed in his best interest. While there was a 30–40 percent chance that chemother-

---

49. *Superintendent of Belchertown State School v. Saikewicz*, 373 Mass. 728 (1977).

apy would produce a remission, it was clear it would not completely cure such leukemia and would involve a great deal of pain. Nevertheless, the evidence before the court suggested that most patients in such condition elect to suffer the side effects of chemotherapy rather than allow their leukemia to run its natural course. It was clear, then, that in a case of an ordinary patient the best interest would be to treat the cancer. The court nevertheless decided that Saikewicz should not be treated.

What the court found as "the most troubling aspect" of offering treatment to Saikewicz was not pain itself, but rather that "if he is treated with toxic drugs he will be involuntarily immersed in a state of painful suffering, *the reason for which he will never understand.* [Competent] patients who request treatment know the risks involved and can appreciate the painful side-effects when they arrive. They know the reason for the pain and their hope makes it tolerable."[50]

This view complicates the Benthamite understanding of pain, but at the same time is captured within its horizon. The court acknowledges that it is not the intensity of pain as such that makes pain intolerable, but rather its senselessness. The problem of pain is not its effect on the senses, but its intelligibility. Pain can be suffered only as long as it can be understood and justified. Since Saikewicz cannot make sense of the pain he will undergo, it would be inhumane to force it upon him. On the other hand, a competent patient may decide to undergo such treatment, for it could be justified in terms of a possible recovery, in which case the suffering would be justified by future gains. Thus, the calculative relation to pain can emerge only on the basis of the more fundamental relation to pain, which is its intelligibility.

One may wish to interpret this phenomenon psychologically. It is a well-established psychological fact that the amount and quality of pain we feel are also determined by our ability to understand the cause of pain and grasp its consequences.[51] In other words, the ability to understand the cause of pain decreases the experience of its intensity. Accordingly, one may wish to argue that Saikewicz, who had no understanding of his pain and its causes, would suffer more than the ordinary patient would.

But, this is not how the court understands the problem of pain, nor

50. Ibid., 750; emphasis added.
51. Melzack and Wall, *The Challenge of Pain*, 15.

should the problem of pain be understood psychologically. The court did not withhold medical treatment from Saikewicz because it believed a certain threshold would be crossed, beyond which pain becomes intolerable. The senselessness of pain makes pain absolute rather than relative and calculable. Only sensible pain can be calculated and measured against its alternatives, and it is only the absolute senselessness of pain that can override the sanctity of life.

Painful Death and Painless Life

In addition to the practices of hastening death that have already been considered, including physician-assisted suicide and the withholding and withdrawing of medical treatment, there is another form of relieving the pain and suffering of dying that should be considered. This practice is known in medical jargon as terminal sedation and is offered to dying patients in the last stages of their disease. Its goal is to overcome the pain and suffering accompanying the final stages of painful diseases such as AIDS and cancer, when other means of pain relief have failed. And, indeed, regular measures of palliative care cannot always relieve pain; specifically, they have limited power to relieve chronic, as opposed to acute, pain.[52] The medical profession and the courts are therefore forced to contemplate more drastic measures than ordinary pain relief. Terminal sedation is one such extreme measure, although it is a routinely practiced medical procedure. High doses of narcotics are given to patients with the intention of ridding them of their pain by putting them into a deep sedation from which they will not awake.

The practice of terminal sedation is especially important because it is commonly offered as an argument against the practice of physician-assisted suicide.[53] There is no need for physician-assisted suicide if pain and suffering can be relieved without killing the patient. And though occasionally the patient does die from terminal sedation within

---

52. "Despite the obvious progress in our knowledge, many people who suffer cancer pain, post-surgical pain, labour pain and various chronic pains are inadequately treated" (Melzack and Wall, *The Challenge of Pain*, x).

53. In the case of *Glucksberg v. Vacco*, mentioned above, O'Connor does not find it necessary to decide whether a right to physician-assisted suicide exists. This is due to the fact that both parties have agreed that in the states of Washington and New York a patient who is suffering from a terminal illness and who is experiencing great pain has no legal barriers to obtaining medication to alleviate that suffering. It is not that the problem of pain has seceded in face of the sanctity of life, but rather that in this case the court prefers a different solution to the problem.

a short time after administration of the drugs, in most cases the patient does not die immediately and may remain in a state of sedation for periods varying from days to weeks and even longer.

Terminal sedation appears to offer a magical remedy to the problem of pain. The patient is hooked to a morphine drip that delivers a constant supply of narcotics and is released from the most torturous experience of pain. We have already come across a similar solution, albeit somewhat primitive, in the writings of Munk on opium. Since Munk's time there have been remarkable innovations in pain control management, but the principle has remained the same: pain accompanying death can and should be eradicated. The courts, along with the medical profession, have recommended the practice of terminal sedation as the ultimate solution to the problem of pain. But can this dream of a painless death devoid of suffering become true? Could this modern fantasy, based on the Benthamite calculus of pain, be realized? Or is the Benthamite calculus of pain flawed and pain in the final analysis central to life, so that a price must be paid for attempting to eradicate it without eradicating life? In answering this question we approach the core of the problem of pain.

Terminal sedation captures at once the victory of modern technology over pain and the Pyrrhic nature of this victory. Using of the most advanced technologies of the day, such as the morphine drip, even the worst pain can be overcome. And yet, once pain has been overcome and the patient has fallen into a deep state of unconsciousness, a new problem arises: namely, is such a life worth living? A patient in terminal sedation cannot sustain himself, so in order to survive he must be connected to feeding tubes and other life-support machinery. It is quite telling that in many cases of terminal sedation, the medical profession decides that there is very little point in maintaining this form of life. The common solution is to withhold or withdraw treatment so the patient dies of dehydration within a few days. This solution has been granted the full support of the law.[54]

Terminal sedation manifests the paradoxical nature of pain. On the one hand, a life accompanied by intolerable suffering is not worth liv-

---

54. The Supreme Court, at least according to Justice O'Connor's opinion, is willing to accept this solution with its problematic consequences. Writing on the availability of medication to alleviate pain, O'Connor writes that both parties agree it may be lawfully administered "even to the point of causing unconsciousness and hastening death" (*Washington v. Glucksberg*, 702). For the medical approach, see Paul Rousseau, "Terminal Sedation in the Care of Dying Patients," *Archival of International Medicine* 156 (1996): 1785.

ing. To make life tolerable pain must be relieved by all available measures, even if the price is a permanent state of unconsciousness. On the other hand, there is a point beyond which the elimination of all pain leads to a life not worth living, as in the case of an unconscious sedated patient. Pain, therefore, becomes that which one cannot live with, nor wish to live without. Living a painless life becomes, in these extreme cases, as problematic as dying a painful death.

The solution the court offers in its most recent decision on physician-assisted suicide brings us back full circle to the case of Karen Quinlan. There is a striking resemblance between the terminally sedated patient and the patient in a persistent vegetative state. In both cases life is viewed as unworthy of prolonging, not because of the suffering of severe pain, but because there is no longer any possibility to experience pain or any other sensation. Here again the calculative approach to pain breaks down. Death is sought not because the balance of pain outweighs that of pleasure, but because we understand that a life without pain is a life without pleasure. Pain and pleasure are not seen as opposites, with pain as life negating and pleasure life affirming; rather, it becomes clear that they belong together and that the annihilation of pain is the annihilation of life itself.

We may wish to return now to the so-called epistemological problem of pain. It is striking that despite our conviction that pain is subjective and known with certainty only to the sufferer, the courts, with the assistance of the medical profession, ground their decisions on a knowledge of pain. Perhaps, after all, pain is not private, and the dichotomy between the subjective experience of pain and its objective knowledge obscures our understanding of pain. The argument that one can only know one's own pain, while others will always remain in doubt regarding this pain, is both false and misleading. Of course one can always doubt whether a patient is indeed suffering from pain, and occasionally within specific contexts this does happen; but in the absence of any substantial reason to doubt it, the pain of others is generally treated by us as real.[55]

---

55. "I can only *believe* that someone else is in pain, but I *know* it if I am."—Yes: one can make the decision to say "I believe he is in pain" instead of "He is in pain." But that is all.—What looks like an explanation here, or like a statement about a mental process, is in truth an exchange of one expression for another which, while we are doing philosophy, seems the more appropriate one. Just try—in a real case—to doubt someone else's fear or pain." Ludwig Wittgenstein, *Philosophical Investigations*, trans. G. E. M. Anscombe (New York: Macmillan, 1953), 102.

Furthermore, treating the problem as an epistemological one, that is, one related to the conditions of knowledge, is misleading. We do not *know* we are in pain, we *have* pain. Likewise, our relation to the pain of others is not by way of knowing it. We do not *know* the pain of others (say, by learning it from their behavior), but primarily *share* with them their pain. (This needs to be understood ontologically rather than morally, and moralizingly.) This is not to deny the existence of the sensation of pain, but only to say that this sensation is always already part of an intelligible world, which can be shared with others. The intersubjective reality of pain is especially noticeable in such cases as that of Conroy and Quinlan, in which decisions are made on the basis of the suffering of the patient, while the patient herself cannot report such suffering, and at least in the case of Quinlan is probably not suffering at all. The place of pain, therefore, is not the private world of the dying patient, but the public realm in which pain can be shared with others. While it is clearly the case that in today's reality of dying the patients have very few occasions to share their pain with significant others, this does not contradict the intersubjective aspect of pain; on the contrary, it only shows the degree to which its lack is noticeable.[56]

To conclude, the right-to-die cases entailing the withholding of medical treatment, the withdrawal of life-support machinery, physician-assisted suicide, and terminal sedation emerge as solutions to the problem of pain. As much as they are about individual autonomy and self-determination, they are also about the intolerable pain that accompanies death. We have seen that underlying the courts' commonsensical understanding of pain lies a deeper, perhaps more essential, understanding of pain. In this understanding the problem of pain is not its intensity but its senselessness; pain is not merely the opposite of pleasure but a condition of life, and death becomes a solution to the problem of pain, when life as well as pain can no longer be justified.

---

56. Hannah Arendt, too, misses the mark on this point, when she speaks of the essential privatized essence of pain: "[I]ndeed, the most intense feeling we know of, intense to the point of blotting out all other experiences, namely, the experience of great bodily pain, is at the same time the most private and least communicable of all. Pain, in other words, truly a borderline experience between life as 'being among men' *(inter homines esse)* and death, is so subjective and removed from the world of things and men that it cannot assume an appearance at all." Hannah Arendt, *The Human Condition* (Chicago: University of Chicago Press, 1958), 51. As we have seen, pain and even bodily pain is not a sign of death, but of life. There is much more validity to her claim, however, if one delimits its scope to the modern age, a time during which pain has indeed lost its public significance.

Neither the problem of pain in dying nor its solution, hastened death, can be understood on the basis of the commonsensical understanding of pain. The problem of pain is not intensity but intelligibility, not sensitivity but sensibility. Death as the solution to the problem of pain is not the rational result of any calculus. The choice of death should be understood as a much more radical rejection not of any particular life in which pain has crossed an unseen threshold of tolerance, but as a cultural response to a deep crisis in the place pain has in modern life. This is so in a world in which the only sense of pain is that given to it by the technology designed to eradicate it, and the only true overcoming of pain is death.

Contributors

Jennifer L. Culbert is Visiting Assistant Professor of Law, Jurisprudence, and Social Thought at Amherst College.

Timothy V. Kaufman-Osborn is Professor of Political Science at Whitman College.

Shai J. Lavi is a graduate student in Jurisprudence and Social Policy at the University of California, Berkeley.

Austin Sarat is William Nelson Cromwell Professor of Jurisprudence and Political Science at Amherst College, former President of the Law and Society Association, and currently President of the Association for the Study of Law, Culture, and the Humanities.

Karl Shoemaker is a graduate student in Jurisprudence and Social Policy at the University of California, Berkeley.

Index